MR 13 '02	DATE DUE		
MY 28 '04			

Science Projects About
Kitchen Chemistry

Titles in the **Science Projects** *series*

Science Projects About
Kitchen Chemistry

Robert Gardner

Science Projects

Enslow Publishers, Inc.

40 Industrial Road   PO Box 38
Box 398   Aldershot
Berkeley Heights, NJ 07922   Hants GU12 6BP
USA   UK
http://www.enslow.com

Library of Congress Cataloging-in-Publication Data

Gardner, Robert, 1929–
    Science projects about kitchen chemistry / by Robert Gardner.
        p. cm. — (Science projects)
    Includes bibliographical references and index.
    Summary: Presents experiments suitable for science fair projects, dealing with the
chemistry involved with foods and activities related to the kitchen.
    ISBN 0-89490-953-3
    1. Chemistry—Experiments—Juvenile literature. [1. Chemistry—Experiments.
2. Experiments. 3. Science projects.] I. Title. II. Series: Gardner, Robert, 1929–
Science projects.
QD38.G382   1999
540'.78—dc21   98-35050
                                                              CIP
                                                              AC

Printed in the United States of America

10 9 8 7 6 5 4 3 2

To Our Readers:
All Internet addresses in this book were active and appropriate when we went to press. Any
comments or suggestions can be sent by e-mail to Comments@enslow.com or to the address
on the back cover.

Illustration Credits: Stephen F. Delisle

Cover Illustration: Jerry McCrea (foreground); © Corel Corporation (background).

Contents

*appropriate ideas for science fair project

*appropriate ideas for science fair project

Introduction

Did you ever think that the foods in your family's kitchen were actually chemicals? You may not think of them that way, but after doing the experiments in this book, you will know that they are. You may not think of a kitchen as a laboratory, but it can be one. A kitchen has a sink where you can get hot and cold water to prepare solutions, a stove where you can heat substances, a refrigerator where you can lower temperatures and keep things cold. There is probably a freezer where you can change many liquids to solids by lowering their temperatures and an exhaust fan (above the stove) to carry away unpleasant odors.

Kitchens also contain a number of instruments that are found in chemistry labs. These include spoons, knives, glass and plastic vessels, measuring cups that can serve as graduated cylinders, filters (usually used for making coffee), funnels, pans in which water can be boiled, and various other useful tools.

For some experiments, you may need more than one pair of hands. When you do, ask friends or family members to help you. Some of the experiments will take some time, so try to choose friends who are patient. If possible, work with someone or some others who share your interest in science. In a few experiments **where there is a potential for danger, you will be asked to work with an adult**. Please do so! The reason for the request is to prevent you from being hurt.

As a good scientist, you will find it useful to record in a notebook your ideas, data, and anything you can conclude from your experiments. By so doing, you can keep track of the information you gather and the conclusions you reach. Using your notebook, you can refer to experiments you have done, and that may help you in doing future projects.

Science Fairs

Some of the projects in this book might be appropriate for a science fair. Those projects are indicated with an asterisk (*). However, judges at such fairs do not reward projects or experiments that are simply copied from a book without any original thinking. For example, a papier-mâché model of a molecule, which is commonly found at these fairs, would probably not impress judges unless it was done in a novel or creative way. On the other hand, a carefully performed series of experiments showing how the acidity or alkalinity (pH) of various foods can be measured using indicators prepared from natural substances found in kitchen chemicals or foods would be likely to receive careful consideration.

Science fair judges tend to reward creative thought and imagination, but it is difficult to be creative or imaginative unless you are really interested in your project. Consequently, if you decide to do a project, choose a topic that appeals to you. Consider, too, your own ability and the cost of materials. Do not pursue a project that requires a graduate degree in chemistry or one that uses materials you cannot afford.

If you decide to use a project found in this book for a science fair, you will need to find ways to modify or extend it. This should not be difficult, because you will probably find that as you do these projects, new ideas for experiments will come to mind. These new experiments could make excellent science fair projects, particularly because they sprang from your own mind and are interesting to you.

If you decide to enter a science fair and have never done so before, you should read some of the books listed in the Further Reading, including *Science Fair Projects—Planning, Presenting, Succeeding*, which is one of the books in this series. The references that deal specifically with science fairs will provide plenty of helpful hints and lots of useful information that will enable you to avoid the pitfalls that sometimes plague first-time entrants. You will learn how to prepare appealing reports that include charts and graphs, how to set up and display your work, how to present your project, and how to relate to judges and visitors.

Safety First

Most of the projects included in this book are perfectly safe. However, the following safety rules are well worth reading before you start any project.

1. Do any experiments or projects, whether from this book or of your own design, under the supervision of a science teacher or other knowledgeable adult.

2. Read all instructions carefully before proceeding with a project. If you have questions, check with your supervisor before going any further.

3. Maintain a serious attitude while conducting experiments. Fooling around can be dangerous to you and to others.

4. Wear approved safety goggles when you are doing anything that might cause injury to your eyes.

5. Do not eat or drink while experimenting.

6. Wash your hands with soap and warm water after handling raw foods such as eggs or meat.

7. Have a first-aid kit nearby while you are experimenting.

8. Do not put your fingers or any object other than properly designed electrical connectors into electrical outlets.

9. Never experiment with household electricity except under the supervision of a knowledgeable adult.

10. Do not touch a lit high-wattage bulb. Lightbulbs produce light, but they also produce heat.

1

Some Chemicals and Foods in the Kitchen

From experience you know that some common solids found in your kitchen, such as sugar, disappear when mixed with water or tea. We say the solid (sugar in this case) is *soluble* in the liquids (water and tea). If little or none of the solid disappears, it is *insoluble*.

When a solid disappears into a liquid, the solid is said to *dissolve* in the liquid to form a solution. The solid that dissolves is called the *solute*. The liquid in which the solute dissolves is called the *solvent*. When sugar dissolves in water, the solute is sugar; the solvent is water.

Since sugar is soluble in water, does that mean it is soluble in other liquids such as alcohol? Does solubility—the amount of solute that dissolves in a fixed amount of solvent—depend on the solute? Does temperature affect the amount of solute that can dissolve in water? How does the density (compactness) of a solution compare with that of the solvent? How does the size of solute particles affect a beam of light? You can find the answers to these questions and many more by doing the experiments found in this chapter.

1-1*
Sugar, Salt, Water: Solutions and the Tyndall Effect

Things you will need:

- teaspoon
- sugar
- small glasses or beakers
- water
- spoon
- iodized salt
- dark area
- penlight or small flashlight
- kosher salt

Pour a teaspoon of sugar into a small glass or beaker. Fill the vessel about halfway with warm water and stir the mixture with a spoon. As you can see, the sugar dissolves in the water to form a solution.

Pour half a teaspoon of ordinary iodized salt into a second small glass or beaker. Fill the glass about halfway with warm water and stir with a spoon. This time the salt also disappears. However, the impurities that were added to the salt when it was iodized result in a very finely divided solid that remains evenly dispersed (spread) throughout the solution.

Take both solutions to a dark area. Use a penlight or a small flashlight to shine a narrow beam of light through the salt solution while you view the liquid from the side, as shown in Figure 1. If you can see the beam in the liquid when you view it from the side, you are observing what is called the Tyndall effect.

The effect is named for John Tyndall (1820–1893), an Irish physicist, who studied it and used it to explain a number of atmospheric phenomena. In clear solutions, no light bounces off the dissolved particles, because they are too small to reflect any light. But larger particles do reflect some light, so a light beam can be seen from the side, just as a beam of sunlight can be seen when it shines through dust particles in a room or through water droplets in the atmosphere.

Is there a Tyndall effect when you shine the light through the sugar solution? Is there a Tyndall effect when you shine the light

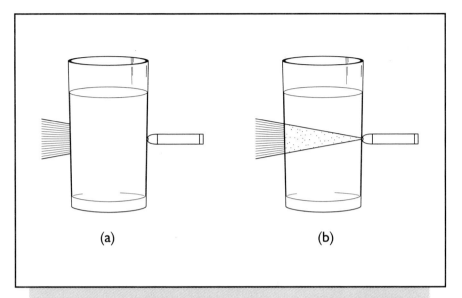

(a)   (b)

Figure 1. a) A beam of light passing through a solution cannot be seen from the side. The dissolved particles are too small to reflect light. b) Larger particles spread throughout a liquid will reflect some light, making the beam visible. This is called the Tyndall effect.

through a glass of ordinary water? Is there a Tyndall effect when you shine the light through a salt solution made by adding kosher salt to water? (Kosher salt does not have the impurities added to iodized salt.)

Exploring on Your Own

Read some descriptions of John Tyndall's work. How did he use the Tyndall effect to explain atmospheric phenomena?

What is iodized salt? What is the reason for adding impurities to ordinary salt, sodium chloride (NaCl)?

13

1-2*
Soluble or Insoluble?

You have seen that sugar and salt are soluble in water. Now try to dissolve 1/4 teaspoon of cornstarch in a small glass or beaker half-filled with water. Stir the mixture with a spoon. What can you say about the solubility of cornstarch in water?

Try dissolving small amounts (about 1/4 teaspoon) of baking soda, baking powder, flour, tooth powder, instant tea, instant coffee, Kool-Aid, Tang, vitamin C, cleansing powder, aspirin, gelatin, and wood ashes, each in half a glass or beaker of water. Which substances are soluble in water? Which are insoluble? Are any of the insoluble substances soluble in hot water?

Things you will need:

- teaspoon
- cornstarch
- small glass or beaker
- cold and hot water
- spoon
- baking soda
- baking powder
- flour
- tooth powder
- instant tea
- instant coffee
- Kool-Aid
- Tang
- vitamin C
- cleansing powder
- aspirin
- gelatin
- wood ashes

Exploring on Your Own

Sometimes substances that are soluble in water can be separated from each other when they move through a solid substance such as paper, because the substances will move at different rates. The process is called *paper chromatography*. To see whether or not different food colorings can be separated by paper chromatography, cut four strips about 2 cm x 15 cm (1 in x 6 in) from coffee filters. Use a fine brush to paint a stripe of food coloring about 2 cm (1 in) from one end of the strip. Rinse the brush in water, then use it to

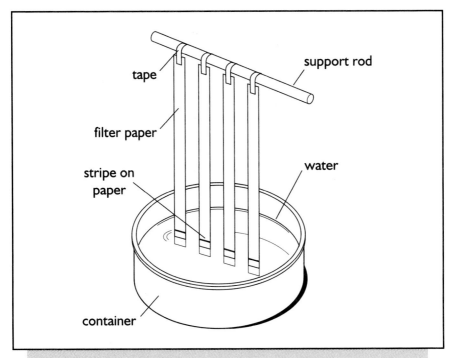

Figure 2. Paper chromatography can often be used to separate similar substances in a mixture.

paint a stripe with a different color. After the colored stripes are dry, hang the paper strips as shown in Figure 2. The bottom ends of the strips should just touch the water in a wide container. What happens as the water climbs the paper? Can paper chromatography be used to separate chemicals in food colorings? Could this method be used with substances that are not soluble in water? Could other solvents be used for substances that are insoluble in water?

1-3*
Saturated Solutions and Solubility

To find out how much salt a given volume of water will hold, pour 100 mL of water from a graduated cylinder or measuring cup into a glass or beaker. Using a balance, weigh out about 50 g of kosher salt. Add a small amount of the salt you weighed to the water. Stir the mixture until the salt dissolves. Continue to add salt in small amounts and stir into solution until no more salt will dissolve. When no additional solute will dissolve in a solvent, we say that the solution is *saturated*.

Weigh the dry salt that remains. Approximately what mass of salt dissolved in the water? The solubility of a solute is the mass of that substance that will dissolve in 100 g of a solvent at a certain temperature. (In the case of water, 100 mL contains 100 g because each milliliter of water has a mass of 1 gram.) What is the approximate solubility of salt in water at room temperature?

In a similar manner, prepare a saturated solution of Epsom salts [magnesium sulfate ($MgSO_4$)] and one of sugar (sucrose). What is the approximate solubility of Epsom salts in water at room temperature? What is the approximate solubility of sugar in water at room temperature? Label and save these saturated solutions for further use.

Pour some of the saturated solution of Epsom salts into another glass or beaker. Do you think any kosher salt will dissolve in the saturated solution of Epsom salts? Add a small amount of the salt and stir. Does the salt dissolve?

Do you think Epsom salts will now dissolve in the saturated salt solution? Test your prediction by adding a small amount of Epsom salts to the solution. Were you right?

Exploring on Your Own

Predict the mass of salt required to prepare a saturated solution using 50 mL of water. Test your prediction. Were you right? Can you predict the amount of salt that will dissolve in 25 mL of water? Since temperature might affect the solubility of these solids, how should the temperature of the two different volumes of water compare?

How does the surface area of a solute affect the rate at which it dissolves? Design an experiment to find out.

What effect does stirring have on the dissolving process? To find out, add a teaspoon of sugar to each of two glasses filled with warm water. Stir one but not the other. In which glass does the sugar dissolve faster? Will the sugar eventually dissolve in both glasses?

A more accurate way to measure solubility is to pour some saturated solution into a saucer or evaporating dish with a known weight. Then weigh the dish and solution to find the mass of the solution.

Place the solution in a warm place so that the water will evaporate. It will leave the dissolved salt behind. After all the water has evaporated and the salt is dry, reweigh the dish. Weigh it several times to be sure that the solid is thoroughly dry and its mass is not changing. How much solid remains?

Knowing the mass of the solution and the mass of the dissolved solid, how can you find the mass of the water in which it was dissolved? How can you determine the solubility of the solid in grams per 100 grams of water?

Use this method to find the mass of table salt (sodium chloride), Epsom salts, and sugar in 100 g of water at room temperature. How do your results compare with your previous measurements of solubility?

1-4*
Solutions, Solvents, and Density

You may have noticed that even though a lot of solute may dissolve in a solvent to form a saturated solution, the volume of the solvent does not increase as much as you might think it would. Does this mean that there is more matter per volume in the solution than there was in the solvent before the solute was added?

To find out, you can measure the density of the solvent, in this case water, and the density of the saturated solutions of salt, sugar, and Epsom salts. Density is a measure of compactness, of the amount of matter in a certain volume. It is found by dividing the mass of any substance by its volume.

To find the density of water, you can first weigh an empty graduated cylinder or metric measuring cup. Then add a convenient volume of water, such as 100 mL, and reweigh. What is the mass of the water? (Do not forget to subtract the mass of the container from the total mass.) Divide the mass of the water by its volume to find its density.

You probably found that 100 mL of water weighs almost exactly 100 g. Therefore, the density of water is

$$100 \text{ g} \div 100 \text{ mL} = 1 \text{ g/mL}.$$

Now find the densities of the saturated solutions of salt, sugar, and Epsom salts. How do the densities of these solutions compare with one another and with that of water?

Exploring on Your Own

The average density of seawater is 1.025 g/mL. Do you think seawater is a saturated salt solution? Why or why not?

1-5*
Precipitation and Precipitates

You have seen solid substances dissolve in water. Now you will see solids appear when solutions are mixed. The solid that forms when two solutions are mixed is called a precipitate. You can obtain a precipitate by mixing solutions that contain soluble substances such as Epsom salts (magnesium sulfate [$MgSO_4$]) and ammonia. Even though both ammonia and Epsom salts are soluble in water, they combine to form magnesium hydroxide, which is insoluble.

To prepare a precipitate of magnesium hydroxide, fill a small glass, beaker, or a test tube about one third of the way with a saturated solution of Epsom salts. **Under adult supervision**, add an equal volume of household ammonia. What happens? Set the glass aside to see if the precipitate will settle to the bottom of the mixture.

Things you will need:

- small glasses, beakers, or test tubes
- saturated solution of Epsom salts
- household ammonia
- an adult
- saturated solution of alum
- saturated solution of washing soda (sodium carbonate) or of a detergent that contains washing soda
- saturated solution of calcium chloride or a salt used to melt ice from sidewalks that contains calcium chloride
- coffee filter
- funnel
- plastic cover from a coffee can
- scissors
- tall glass, jar, or beaker

It may take a day or two to find out whether or not the precipitate will settle. Meanwhile, prepare a saturated solution of alum—potassium aluminum sulfate ($KAl[SO_4]_2$). To about one third of a glassful of the saturated alum solution, add an equal volume of household ammonia, as before, **under adult supervision**. How does this precipitate, which is aluminum hydroxide, compare with magnesium hydroxide?

Another precipitate that can be obtained from kitchen chemicals is calcium carbonate ($CaCO_3$). Calcium carbonate is the main component in the shells of sea-dwelling organisms and the eggshells of birds. To make this precipitate, you will need to prepare saturated solutions of washing soda, which is sodium carbonate (Na_2CO_3), and calcium chloride ($CaCl_2$). Calcium chloride is the main component in some salts used to melt ice from sidewalks and driveways. If you cannot find pure washing soda, you can use a detergent that lists sodium carbonate as an ingredient. Mix equal volumes of these two saturated solutions and observe the precipitate that forms. What color is it?

How do the densities of the precipitates you have prepared compare with the densities of the solutions in which they form? Why is this? Other than water, what substances do you think would be found in each of the solutions in which you saw precipitates forming?

To separate a precipitate, such as magnesium hydroxide, from the solution in which it formed, you can filter the mixture of precipitate and solution. A filter can be made by folding a coffee filter and placing it in a funnel (Figure 3a). If necessary, the funnel can be supported by a plastic cover from a coffee can, or it can rest on the top of a jar. A circle cut from the center of the cover (Figure 3b) will allow part of the body of the funnel to pass through so that the stem of the funnel is in a tall glass, jar, or beaker. Let the filtrate (the liquid that comes through the filter) collect in the tall vessel (Figure 3c). Where do you find the precipitate?

Let the solid magnesium hydroxide on the filter paper dry. You can use some of it for your next experiment. Save the rest for use in Experiment 3-1.

Exploring on Your Own

Although we say that precipitates such as magnesium hydroxide are insoluble in water, they are really slightly soluble. Design and carry out an experiment to find the actual solubility of magnesium hydroxide in grams per 100 grams of water.

20

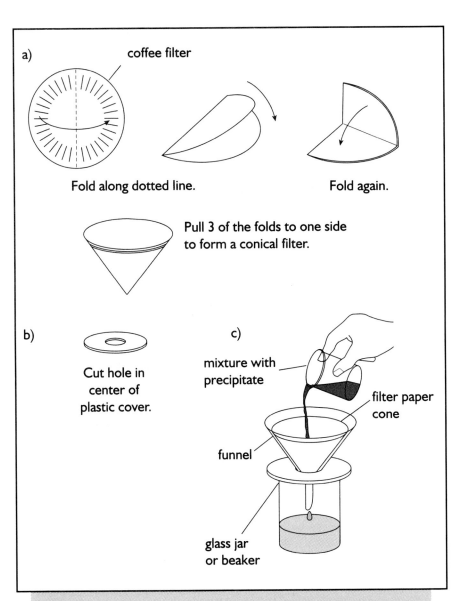

a) coffee filter

Fold along dotted line.   Fold again.

Pull 3 of the folds to one side to form a conical filter.

b) Cut hole in center of plastic cover.

c) mixture with precipitate

filter paper cone

funnel

glass jar or beaker

Figure 3. A precipitate can be separated from the solution in which it formed by filtering the mixture into a tall glass, jar, or beaker. a) Convert a coffee filter to a cone-shaped filter by folding twice and opening, as shown. b) If necessary, cut a hole in a plastic cover to support the funnel. c) Place the conical filter into the funnel and pour in the mixture of solution and precipitate.

1-6*
Does Temperature Affect Solubility?

Things you will need:

- graduated cylinder or metric measuring cup
- hot water
- glass or beaker
- large pan
- spoon or other stirring instrument
- kosher salt
- Epsom salts
- sugar

In Experiment 1-3, you measured the solubility of table salt and Epsom salts in water at room temperature. To find out whether or not temperature affects solubility, you can measure the solubility of salt, Epsom salts, and sugar in hot water.

Add 50 mL of hot tap water to a glass or beaker. Place the vessel in a large pan of hot water so that the temperature of the solvent will not change as you add solute and stir the solution. What is the solubility of salt in hot water? (Express solubility in grams of solute per 100 grams of solvent.) What is the solubility of Epsom salts in hot water? Of sugar in hot water? Does temperature affect solubility? For which of the solutes you tested was solubility affected most by temperature?

Exploring on Your Own

Design an experiment to find the temperature at which water and saturated solutions of salt and Epsom salts freeze. How do the freezing temperatures of these liquids compare?

Do you think a bouillon cube will dissolve faster in hot water or in cold water? Design and carry out an experiment to find out.

It is possible to determine the solubility of various salts at different temperatures, but it is not easy to do without a laboratory where temperatures can be controlled. Figure 4 is a graph showing the solubility of several salts at different temperatures. Use the graph

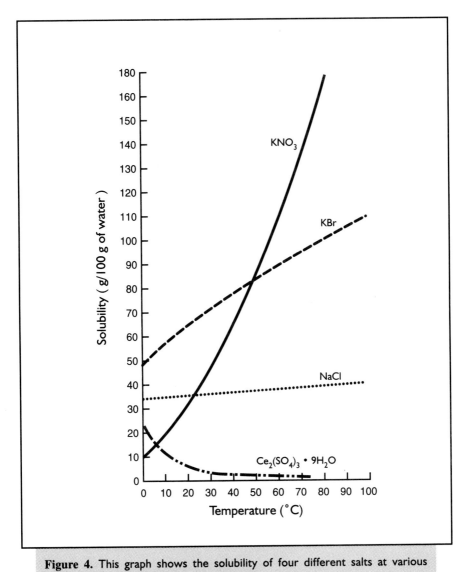

Figure 4. This graph shows the solubility of four different salts at various temperatures. KNO_3 = potassium nitrate
$NaCl$ = sodium chloride
KBr = potassium bromide
$Ce_2(SO_4)_3 \cdot 9H_2O$ = cerium sulfate hydrate

to find the solubilities of sodium chloride and potassium nitrate at different temperatures. What do you notice about their comparative solubilities?

Which salt in Figure 4 is least soluble at room temperature? Which salt shows the greatest increase in solubility with temperature? For which salt does solubility decrease as the temperature rises?

1-7
Solvents Other than Water

Water is not the only liquid that can be used as a solvent. Some substances that are not soluble in water are soluble in other liquids such as alcohol. Alcohol is often used as a solvent for things that will not dissolve in water.

Ask your science teacher if you may have a few milliliters of methanol. **Caution! Methanol, also known as wood alcohol, is poisonous and flammable. With an adult's help** add a pinch of sugar to 10 mL of methanol. Stir or shake the mixture. Is sugar soluble in methanol?

With an adult to help you, use a wooden coffee stirrer to add a few crystals of moth flakes to 10 mL of methanol. Add a similar amount of moth flakes to 10 mL of water. Stir both mixtures. Are moth flakes soluble in methanol? Are they soluble in water?

Things you will need:

• methanol
• an adult
• sugar
• moth flakes
• water
• wooden coffee stirrer
• teaspoon
• salt
• baking soda
• baking powder
• flour
• tooth powder
• cornstarch
• instant tea
• instant coffee
• Kool-Aid
• soapy water
• cooking oil
• vinegar
• medicine cup, test tube, or transparent vial

You can try dissolving small amounts—1/10 teaspoonful—of solids (solutes) such as sugar, salt, baking soda, baking powder, flour, tooth powder, cornstarch, instant tea or coffee, and Kool-Aid or other crystals used to make cold drinks in various liquids. For liquids (solvents), you might try soapy water (which you can make from liquid detergent and water), cooking oil, and vinegar. Which of the solids are soluble in soapy water? In cooking oil? In vinegar? What happens when you add baking soda to vinegar? Which of the solids are insoluble in the various liquids?

1-8
Liquids in Liquids

Pour some water into a small glass or beaker. Add about the same amount of rubbing alcohol and stir. Do alcohol and water mix to form a single phase? That is, does the mixture appear to be the same throughout?

Repeat the experiment with water and cooking oil. Do cooking oil and water mix to form a single phase?

Liquids that dissolve in one another are said to be *miscible*. Liquids that do not dissolve in one another are said to be *immiscible*. Which of the liquids you just mixed are miscible? Which are immiscible?

Things you will need:

• water

• small glass or beaker

• rubbing alcohol

• spoon or other stirring device

• cooking oil

• clock or watch with second hand or mode

• liquid detergent

• eyedropper

• vial or test tube

• molasses

• small, tall jar

Half fill a glass, beaker, or test tube with tap water. Add a few drops of cooking oil to the water. How can you tell that cooking oil is less dense than water? Stir or shake the mixture and measure the time it takes for the two liquids to separate into two distinct phases.

Next, add a few drops of liquid detergent to the mixture and stir or shake. Again, measure the time it takes for the two liquids to separate into distinct phases. How does the detergent affect the rate at which the oil separates from the water? Why are detergents used to wash clothes?

Pour some rubbing alcohol into a glass or beaker. Add a few milliliters of cooking oil. Which liquid is more dense? How can you tell?

Using an eyedropper, try to make three distinct liquid layers of alcohol, cooking oil, and water in a vial or test tube. Does it matter

27

in what order you add the liquids to the container? Which liquid forms the bottom layer? Which liquid is on top? How do the densities of water, cooking oil, and alcohol compare? How can you determine the actual density of these liquids?

In a small, tall jar, make three liquid layers, one atop the other, using water, cooking oil, and molasses. Which is the densest of these three liquids? Which is the least dense? Do you think any of the layers will eventually merge? Leave the jar for a few days. Was your prediction correct?

You have seen that a liquid can dissolve in another liquid. Can you show that gases also dissolve in liquids? Can you show that the solubility of a gas such as carbon dioxide in a liquid is affected by temperature? What evidence can you offer to show that gases dissolve in gases?

1-9*
Exploring Emulsions

Find a small jar with a screw-on lid that is taller than it is wide. Add vinegar to the jar until it is about 1/8 full. Then add about twice as much cooking oil. Do vinegar and cooking oil appear to be miscible?

Put the lid on the jar and shake it so as to break up the liquids and mix them together. Notice how tiny droplets of cooking oil spread throughout the liquid. Such a mixture is called an emulsion. Oil spills in the ocean are difficult to clean up because the wind and waves mix oil and seawater, forming an emulsion.

Let the emulsion sit for a few minutes. What happens to the two liquids over time? Why is this mixture called a temporary emulsion?

Next, separate the yolk of an egg from the white. Crack the egg at its center with a table knife. Hold the egg upright over a cereal bowl and remove the upper half of the shell. Some egg white will fall into the bowl when you remove the upper half of the shell. Then carefully pour the yolk, trying not to break it, from one half of the shell to the other several times over the bowl. As you do so, more egg white will fall into the bowl. When most of the white has been removed, pour the yolk into the mixture of oil and vinegar, put the lid on the jar, and shake it again. Let this mixture sit for a few minutes. Is this a more permanent emulsion? Why do you think the egg yolk is called an emulsifying agent? Test other foods in your refrigerator to find an even more permanent emulsion. **Always wash your hands with soap and warm water after handling raw eggs.**

Exploring on Your Own

Mayonnaise, which is an emulsion, can be made from salad oil, vinegar, and some spices using egg yolks as an emulsifying agent.

Find a recipe for making mayonnaise and try to make some. Be careful to add the oil very slowly as you mix the ingredients so that the egg yolk can coat the droplets and prevent them from coming back together.

A suspension is a mixture that contains small particles of an insoluble solid dispersed through a liquid. You can make a very interesting suspension by putting 125 mL (1/2 cup) of cornstarch into a bowl and adding half as much water. Mix the solid and liquid together with your hands. What happens when you try to squeeze a handful of the stuff? Try to pick up the mixture using a spoon. Put some of the suspension on a flat surface. What happens to it? Punch a small hole in a piece of paper and put some of the mixture over the hole. Does it leak through? What other properties do you notice about this strange stuff?

1-10
Three Cleaning Solutions

Find three old copper pennies that have lost their luster and are dull. What do you think is the dark film on the pennies?

Place the pennies in separate medicine cups or small dishes as shown in Figure 5. To one penny add some vinegar. To a second penny add a solution of salt and water. To the remaining penny add vinegar and salt. Using masking tape and a pen, label the three containers so that you can identify them. Watch the pennies over the course of several days.

Things you will need:

* 3 old copper pennies
* 3 small cups or dishes
* vinegar
* salt
* water
* masking tape
* pen

Do all the pennies regain their luster? Why does the dark material on the pennies disappear? Which cleaner works fastest?

dull penny

vinegar   salt and water   vinegar and salt

Figure 5. Three different cleaning liquids are added to separate pennies. Which cleaner works best? Which cleaner works fastest?

2

The Three Basic Foods

Unlike green plants, humans and other animals cannot manufacture their own food from water and carbon dioxide. The energy we need to live must come from the food we eat. There are three basic foods: carbohydrates, fats, and proteins. Of course, we also need a variety of minerals and vitamins as well, but this chapter will focus on the basic foods from which we obtain our energy.

Carbohydrates

Carbohydrates, as their name implies, contain only three elements: carbon, hydrogen, and oxygen. The basic carbohydrates are simple sugars such as glucose and fructose, whose molecules contain 6 carbon atoms, 12 hydrogen atoms, and 6 oxygen atoms and can be represented by the formula $C_6H_{12}O_6$. Both glucose and fructose have the same chemical formula. They differ only in the way the atoms are arranged within the molecules.

As you probably know, *mono* means one and *di* means two. Disaccharides consist of the union of two simple sugar molecules (monosaccharides; see Figure 6). During the union, a molecule of

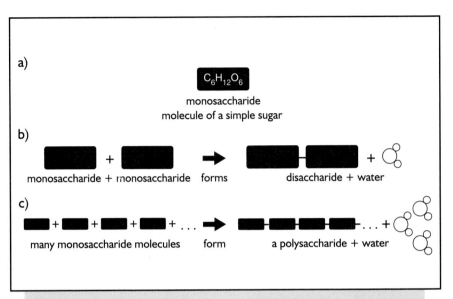

Figure 6. a) Monosaccharide molecules, represented here as rectangles, are simple sugars such as glucose and fructose. Each molecule contains 6 carbon atoms, 12 hydrogen atoms, and 6 oxygen atoms. The molecule is represented by the formula $C_6H_{12}O_6$. b) Two monosaccharide molecules can combine to form a single disaccharide molecule and a water molecule (H_2O). c) Many monosaccharide molecules can combine to form large polysaccharide molecules of starch or cellulose and water.

water (H_2O) splits off, so the formula for a disaccharide is $C_{12}H_{22}O_{11}$. The white crystalline compound we commonly call sugar is sucrose, a disaccharide. Other disaccharides include lactose (milk sugar) and maltose (malt sugar).

The union of many monosaccharide units gives rise to polysaccharide molecules. Cellulose, which is the main material in the cell walls of plants and makes up 60 percent of wood, is a polysaccharide. Starches are also polysaccharides.

Our diet normally contains many carbohydrates from bread, potatoes, vegetables, milk, and other dairy products. However, only monosaccharides such as glucose and fructose can pass through our intestinal walls and reach our bloodstreams. Fortunately, enzymes produced in our mouths, stomachs, and intestines can break starches and disaccharides into the monosaccharides glucose and fructose. In the cells of our bodies, glucose and fructose are slowly broken down during a series of chemical reactions to form carbon dioxide (CO_2) and water. These reactions produce the energy we need to keep on living.

Fats and Oils

Like carbohydrates, fats and oils contain only carbon, hydrogen, and oxygen, but not in the same ratio as carbohydrates. Fats and oils are made by the union of glycerol, a sweet, syrupy alcohol commonly known as glycerin, which is found in candies and cough medicine, and fatty acids such as acetic acid, the acid found in vinegar (see Figure 7a). If the product is a solid, it is referred to as fat; if it is a liquid, it is called an oil. These oils should not be confused with lubricating oils, which are hydrocarbons (compounds that contain only carbon and hydrogen).

Fats, which are found in oils, fatty meats such as bacon, egg yolks, nuts, and dairy products, are broken into fatty acids and glycerol in our intestines before being absorbed into our blood. Fats provide twice as much energy per gram as carbohydrates. People whose lifestyles require lots of energy, such as Eskimos living in cold climates, include a lot of fat in their diet.

Proteins

Fat molecules are large, and the molecules of starches are considerably larger, but proteins are the largest of all food molecules. Protein molecules, which are found in eggs, wheat, milk, meat, fish, and vegetables, particularly peas, beans, lentils, and peanuts, contain thousands of atoms. The basic building blocks of proteins are amino acids, which always contain nitrogen as well as carbon, hydrogen, and oxygen; often sulfur; and sometimes phosphorus.

34

Proteins are made up of long chains of 100 or more amino acids (see Figure 7b). In our stomachs and intestines, proteins are digested—broken into amino acids that can be absorbed by our bloodstreams. There are approximately 80 amino acids that occur in nature. Humans require 20 of these acids to build body cells and carry on life-sustaining functions. Human cells can manufacture 9 amino acids from other foods and minerals. The remaining 11, called essential amino acids, must be obtained from the animal or plant tissues in our diet. Since these acids are found in different foods, we require a varied diet to obtain all the amino acids we need. A common cause of malnutrition is having available only one type of food such as rice, which lacks some essential amino acids.

Collagen is one of the most abundant proteins found in animals. It is the major component of the connective tissue fibers found in skin, tendons, and bones. By heating and adding acids, collagen is

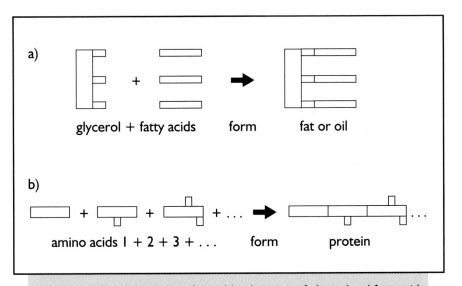

a)

glycerol + fatty acids   form   fat or oil

b)

amino acids I + 2 + 3 + ...   form   protein

Figure 7. a) Fat molecules are formed by the union of glycerol and fatty acid molecules. During digestion, the reverse occurs: Fats are broken down into glycerol and fatty acids. b) Proteins are formed by the union of many molecules of different amino acids. During digestion, protein molecules are broken down into amino acids, which can be absorbed into the bloodstream.

cured, and gelatin, a protein with somewhat smaller molecules, is extracted by boiling.

Commercial gelatin is virtually colorless, odorless, and tasteless. It is insoluble in cold water. Nevertheless, it can absorb up to eight times its own weight of water. Large quantities of gelatin are used to enclose drugs, vitamins, and various medicines in capsules. It is also used in the photographic industry, but its widest use is in the flavored powders used as desserts and salads and in ice cream, where it reduces the growth of ice crystals. It is also an ingredient of marshmallows and is used in preparing jellied meats.

Other Chemicals Needed for Life

In addition to carbohydrates, fats, and proteins, our diets must contain small quantities of essential minerals such as calcium and phosphorus for bones and teeth, iron for blood and other cell functions, iodine for the thyroid gland, plus copper, magnesium, zinc, and trace amounts of a number of other elements. We also need small amounts of vitamins—chemical compounds essential to life, most of which we cannot synthesize ourselves. When vitamins were first discovered, their exact chemical compositions were not known, so they were simply referred to by letters: vitamin A, vitamin B, vitamin C, and so on.

In the late nineteenth century, Christiaan Eijkman was investigating beriberi, a disease of the nervous system that causes paralysis. Quite by accident he discovered that chickens fed polished rice developed symptoms very similar to beriberi. Chickens that were fed whole rice failed to develop the disease. Early in the twentieth century, Frederick Hopkins recognized that there were substances essential to life found in some foods and not others. He suggested that beriberi, along with scurvy and rickets, might be caused by the lack of essential chemicals in the diet. This idea later became known as the vitamin concept. The substance found in the husks of rice that prevented the onset of beriberi became known as vitamin B.

Scurvy, a disease characterized by weakness and bleeding beneath the skin, was associated with a lack of an unknown chemical referred to as vitamin C. Eating citrus fruits, it was found, could cure scurvy. Consequently, these fruits were recognized as a good source of vitamin C.

Rickets, a disease associated with defective bone growth, was found to be caused by a lack of vitamin D. A diet that included small amounts of cod liver oil could prevent rickets. Later, vitamins B1, C, and D were found to be specific chemical substances; namely, thiamine, ascorbic acid, and calciferol.

2-1*
Nutritional Research

Using your school or local library and the Internet, if you have access to it, you can do a number of research projects

Things you will need:
- library
- Internet (optional)

involving foods and nutrition. A few are listed below, but you may find other food topics that are more interesting to you.

What are the daily energy (Calorie) requirements that a normal diet should meet? How much of that energy should come from carbohydrates? From fats? From proteins? Is the energy per mass the same for all three basic foods, or do they differ?

Prepare a month's worth of menus for a variety of people such as an athlete, an office worker, a carpenter, a farmer, or a person who loads ships.

What are the dangers of a high-fat diet? Should people who are overweight try to eliminate fat entirely from their diets?

Investigate the history behind each of the vitamins nutritionists believe are essential parts of a human diet. What is meant by fat-soluble and water-soluble vitamins? Which vitamins, if any, can humans manufacture from other components in their diets? Which vitamins are associated in some way with sunlight?

Marathon runners and other endurance athletes often talk about carbohydrate loading prior to a competition. What is carbohydrate loading? How does it help these athletes? Would it help sprinters? Would it help you?

Why do some people gain weight even when they eat very little, while others can eat and eat and never gain weight? Can a person change this aspect of him- or herself?

Are the artificial ingredients added to some foods dangerous to your health?

Are sweets, such as candy, really harmful to you? If so, in what way are they harmful?

Exploring on Your Own

Find the percentage of carbohydrate, fat, and protein in a variety of common foods. Determine the energy that can be obtained from one gram of each of these foods.

How can diet affect your dental health?

How can exercise bring about weight loss?

2-2*
The Energy Stored in a Peanut

Things you will need:
- small (6-oz) frozen juice can with a metal bottom and cardboard sides
- measuring cup or graduated cylinder
- large nail
- pencil
- large metal can
- can opener
- cork
- aluminum foil
- pliers
- large sewing needle
- balance or scale
- cold water
- thermometer (-10–110°C)
- an adult
- matches
- peanuts
- pencil or pen and paper

When you eat a peanut, it is digested, absorbed into your blood, and carried to cells where it is oxidized slowly in a series of chemical reactions. These reactions release the energy that was stored in the peanut. You can find the energy stored in a peanut or in any other food by burning it in air or oxygen and measuring the energy released.

To find the energy stored in a peanut, you can build a simple calorimeter like the one shown in Figure 8. A small (6-oz) frozen juice can with a metal bottom and cardboard sides can be used to hold 100 g of cold water. **Ask an adult** to use a nail to punch holes through opposite sides of the can, near the top. Then push a long pencil through the holes. The pencil will be used to support this small can on a larger one.

Find a large, clean metal can. **Ask an adult** to make four or five triangular holes along the sides of the can near its bottom and then remove both ends of the can, as shown in Figure 8. The holes will allow air to enter the can so that the peanut will burn. The shiny interior of the large can will reflect heat that might otherwise escape to the surrounding air.

To support the peanut, cover the small end of a cork with a piece of aluminum foil. Use pliers to force the eye of a large sewing

40

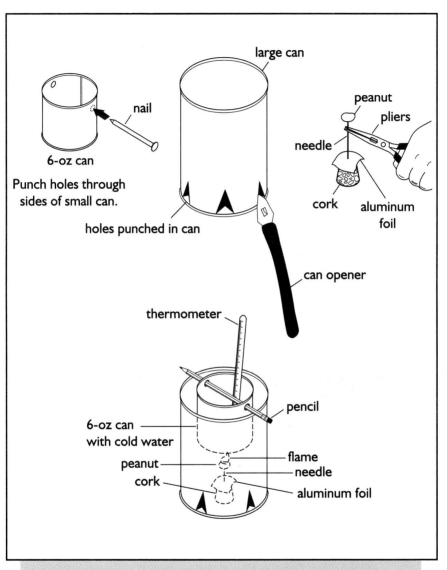

large can

nail

6-oz can

Punch holes through
sides of small can.

holes punched in can

peanut

pliers

needle

cork

aluminum
foil

can opener

thermometer

pencil

6-oz can
with cold water

peanut

cork

flame

needle

aluminum foil

Figure 8. A calorimeter to measure the heat released by a peanut can be made
from two cans, a cork, aluminum foil, water, a needle, and a thermometer.

needle through the foil and into the cork, as shown. Next, weigh the peanut and place it on the sharp end of the upright needle. Pour 100 g of water into the small can. Since the density of water is 1 g/mL, you can simply measure out a volume of 100 mL (3.5 oz) of cold water and pour it into the can. Place a thermometer in the can and measure the water's temperature.

Ask an adult to light the peanut with a match. Then immediately place the large can over the burning peanut and put the small can with the water into the large can, as shown in Figure 8. Stir the water gently with the thermometer until the peanut goes out.

Record the final temperature of the water. The mass of water and its temperature change can be used to calculate the heat released by the burning peanut. A calorie is the amount of heat required to raise the temperature of 1 gram of water by 1°C. If the temperature of the 100 g of water increased by 10°C, then the peanut provided 1,000 calories (100 g x 10°C) of energy. How much heat, in calories, did the burning peanut release?

If any of the peanut remains, weigh it. What mass of peanut, in grams, provided the heat absorbed by the water? How much heat per gram of peanut burned was released? Do you think the value of the heat per gram that you obtained from your data is higher or lower than the actual value? What makes you think so?

Nutritionists measure energy in what are called large calories or Calories. A Calorie with a capital *C* is the heat needed to raise the temperature of 1 *kilogram* of water by 1C, so it is 1,000 times bigger than a calorie with a small *c*. According to your data, how many Calories are provided by 1 gram of peanut?

Exploring on Your Own

With **an adult to help you**, try measuring the Calories per gram released by other substances, such as walnuts and cashews. How do they compare with peanuts? How could you use this experiment to measure the energy released per gram of candle wax?

2-3*
Fatty Food

Things you will need:

- brown paper bag
- cooking oil
- water
- bacon
- hot dog
- peanut butter
- butter
- margarine
- lard
- milk
- walnut
- cream
- orange juice
- lemonade
- mayonnaise
- low-fat mayonnaise
- egg white
- egg yolk

Chemists have ways of testing for fats, but the techniques involve substances that can be explosive or toxic. There is, however, one simple test that can be used to identify many fatty or oily foods. Tear off one side of a brown paper bag. Put a drop of cooking oil on your finger and rub it in circular fashion on one small section of the brown paper. Use another finger to rub some water into the paper in the same way. If you hold the paper up to a light, you will see that the spot made with the cooking oil and, perhaps, the one made with water as well, are translucent—they transmit light. The liquids transmit light because they fill in the spaces between the wood fibers in the paper. The water spot will become opaque as the liquid evaporates, but the oily spot, which contains fat, will remain translucent.

Try testing some other substances. Make circles in the brown paper, using bacon and the cut side of a hot dog. Try peanut butter, ordinary butter, margarine, and lard. Also try milk, a walnut, cream, orange juice, lemonade, mayonnaise, low-fat mayonnaise, an egg white, and an egg yolk. Which of these substances give a positive test for fat? Which appear to have little or no fat?

Exploring on Your Own

Put a drop of cooking oil on your finger and make a circular spot on a piece of a brown paper bag. Notice that if you hold the spot between your eye and a bright light, the spot is much brighter than the paper. The oil transmits light and the paper does not. When you stand with the light behind you and look at the spot, the spot will appear darker than the paper. Why is this?

The oily spot on the brown paper can be used as a simple photometer. A photometer is a device that can be used to compare the brightness of two light sources.

To see how you can use an oily spot as a photometer, tear off a square piece of paper about 5 cm (2 in) on a side from a brown paper bag. Make a small spot on the paper, as you did before, using cooking oil. Next, place a lamp with a 100-W bulb and a lamp with a 40-W or a 60-W bulb at opposite ends of a long table in an otherwise dark room (see Figure 9). Move the paper slowly back and

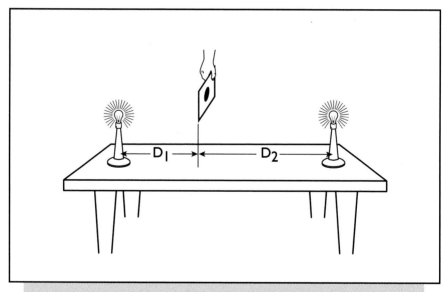

Figure 9. When the intensity of light on the fat spot from the two light sources is equal, what is the distance D_1? What is the distance D_2?

44

forth between the two lights. You will find a point where the spot, when viewed from one side, suddenly changes from dark to light or light to dark. Can you explain why it changes?

If you view the spot from the other side, you will see it change in the same way at the same point. This tells you that at that point, the intensity of the two lights is the same.

Where is that point in your experiment? Since the 100-W bulb is brighter than the 60-W or 40-W bulb, you will probably find the point of equal brightness is nearer the lower-wattage bulb than the 100-W bulb. As you can see in Figure 10, the intensity of a light decreases with the square of its distance from the light source. If you double your distance from a light, the light becomes not half as bright but one fourth as bright, because it is spread over four

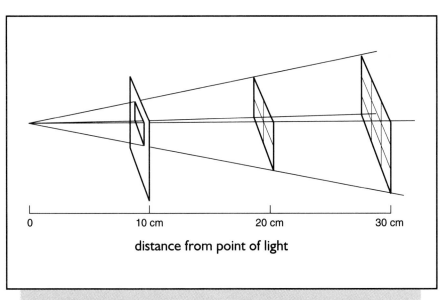

0   10 cm   20 cm   30 cm

distance from point of light

Figure 10. Light from a point source passes through a square opening that is 10 cm from the light. When the same light is 20 cm from its source, it spreads over an area four times the size of the square hole. Consequently, its intensity is one fourth as great as it was 10 cm from the source. At 30 cm from its source, the light covers nine times as much area, so its intensity is only one ninth as great as it was at 10 cm.

times as much area. The intensity of the light from a small light source is inversely proportional to the distance from the source:

$$\text{Intensity} = \frac{\text{constant}}{(\text{distance})^2}$$

Why is the light intensity one ninth as great when the distance from the light source is tripled?

If light intensity is equal when the photometer is 50 cm from the brighter light and 30 cm from the dimmer light, then the relative brightness of the two lights is $5^2 \div 3^2$, or 25/9. What is the relative brightness of the two bulbs you used?

2-4
Carbohydrates

Testing for Starch

In a medicine cup or small container, mix about 10 drops of tincture of iodine with 100 drops of water. **Be careful handling iodine. It is a poison.** You can use this iodine solution to test for starch. To see the distinct color that forms when the iodine comes in contact with starch, mix 1/4 teaspoon of cornstarch with some water in another medicine cup or small container. Use an eyedropper to add a drop of the iodine solution to the starch-water mixture. What color appears when iodine is added to starch? Close the iodine container and put it away.

Now use what you have learned to test a number of different foods for starch. In separate dishes, crush or pour samples of potato, bread, milk, meat, and unsalted cracker. Into still another container, spit a piece of another unsalted cracker that you have chewed for about five minutes.

Mix each of these food samples with a little water. Then test each sample with a drop of the iodine solution. **Remember not to put anything with iodine on it into your mouth!**

Which foods contain starch? What other foods might you try?

Things you will need:
- medicine cups or small containers
- eyedropper
- tincture of iodine
- water
- teaspoon
- cornstarch
- potato
- bread
- milk
- meat
- unsalted crackers
- Clinistix sugar indicators (from a drugstore) or Benedict's solution (from school)
- corn or maple syrup
- test tube or a small glass
- small cooking pan
- an adult
- stove
- sucrose (table sugar)
- saucers
- toothpick

Testing for Sugar

If you can obtain Clinistix sugar indicators from a drugstore, you can use them to test for simple sugars. Just dip the stick in a sample of liquid that you think may contain simple sugars. If Clinistix indicators are not available, your school may have Benedict's solution. **With your teacher's permission and supervision**, you can use Benedict's solution to test for simple sugars. Pour about 5 mL of corn or maple syrup into a test tube or a small glass. Add about 5 mL of the Benedict's solution and place the tube or glass in a small pan that holds some water. Place the pan on a stove and heat the water to boiling. If a simple (monosaccharide) sugar is present, the liquid will turn green, yellow, red, or orange. An orange color indicates a high concentration of simple sugar.

Repeat the experiment, using 5 mL of a saturated solution of sucrose (table sugar). Does this sugar solution contain any simple sugars?

In separate dishes, crush samples of potato, bread, milk, and meat. Into another dish spit an unsalted cracker that you have chewed for about five minutes. Mix each of these samples with a little water and test with Clinistix or Benedict's solution as you did previously.

Mix 1/4 teaspoon of cornstarch with an equal amount of corn or maple syrup, which, as you know from an earlier test, contains a simple sugar. Add some water and stir the mixture with a toothpick. Pour a small amount of the mixture onto a saucer and add a drop of iodine solution. **Remember iodine is poisonous!** Do you get a positive test for starch when it is mixed with sugar? Test for a simple sugar with Clinistix sugar indicators or, **under your teacher's supervision**, test using Benedict's solution. Do you get a positive test for a simple sugar when it is mixed with starch?

2-5
Decomposing Carbohydrates

Chemists often find out what a compound is made of by decomposing it (breaking it up) into simpler substances. As you know, carbohydrates are molecules with three kinds of atoms—carbon, hydrogen, and oxygen. What do you think will happen if you try to decompose carbohydrates by heating them?

You can make a number of small pans with handles by folding pieces of heavy-duty aluminum foil, as shown in Figure 11a. A clothespin can be used to clasp the pan's handle. Place a very small amount of table sugar (sucrose) in one of the pans you made. **Under adult supervision and while wearing safety glasses and an oven mitt**, heat the sugar with a candle that is supported by a candleholder, as shown in Figure 11b.

Things you will need:

- heavy-duty aluminum foil
- clothespin
- table sugar (sucrose)
- an adult
- safety glasses
- oven mitt
- candle and candleholder
- matches
- cornstarch
- flour
- bread
- potato
- corn syrup
- unflavored gelatin
- fine paintbrush
- lemon juice
- paper
- lightbulb

What happens to the sugar when you heat it? Is there any evidence of steam? Does the sugar appear to decompose? Does it eventually turn black? What, do you think, is the black substance?

Repeat the experiment, using a very small amount of cornstarch. What happens to the cornstarch when you heat it?

Try heating very small amounts of other carbohydrates and carbohydrate-rich foods such as flour, bread, raw potato, and a drop

49

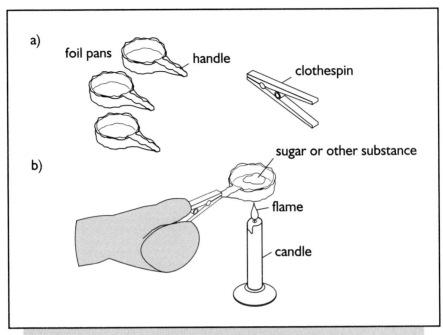

Figure 11. a) Small pans can be made by folding heavy-duty aluminum foil. A clothespin can be used to grasp the handles of these pans. b) Small samples of various carbohydrates can be heated over a candle flame.

of corn syrup. What appears to be the common substance that remains after all these carbohydrates are heated?

To see whether decomposition is limited to carbohydrates, add a few crystals of unflavored gelatin, which is a protein, to one of your aluminum pans. (Save the rest of the gelatin for Experiments 2-10 and 2-11.) Heat the protein with the candle flame. Does the gelatin protein decompose in a way that is similar to the decomposition of carbohydrates?

The decomposition of food when heated is the secret of many invisible inks. Use a fine brush dipped in lemon juice to write a message on a piece of paper. After the invisible ink has dried, heat the paper by holding it above and near, but not touching, an incandescent lightbulb. Why does the message slowly appear?

2-6
Proteins

The Biuret test can be used to identify protein in food. Because the test involves the use of a sodium hydroxide (lye) solution, which is harmful to skin and eyes, you will need **an adult to help you** with this experiment. Both you and the adult should wear safety glasses and rubber gloves throughout the experiment. **The adult** should prepare the sodium hydroxide (NaOH) solution by adding 10 g of the white solid to 90 g of cold water and stirring until the solid is dissolved.

While the adult is preparing the sodium hydroxide solution, you can prepare a 3 percent solution of copper sulfate by adding 3 g of blue copper sulfate ($CuSO_4 \cdot 5H_2O$) crystals to 100 g (100 mL) of water.

Egg white is a good source of protein. It can be used to reveal what a positive test for protein looks like. Separate the white of an egg from its yolk as described in Experiment 1-9. Pour the egg white into a measuring cup and then into a large test tube. **Wash your hands with soap and warm water after handling raw eggs**. Add an equal volume of water. Stopper the tube and shake it to thoroughly mix the egg white and water. **Have the adult** add an equal volume of the sodium hydroxide

Things you will need:

- an adult
- safety glasses
- rubber gloves
- balance
- sodium hydroxide crystals
- cold water
- copper sulfate crystals
- an egg
- metric measuring cup or graduated cylinder
- large test tube
- stopper
- eyedropper
- flour
- gelatin
- potato
- bread
- milk
- meat
- crackers
- sugar

solution. Stopper and shake the tube again. Next, add about 5 drops of the copper sulfate solution. Stopper and shake once more. A violet or blue-violet color indicates the presence of protein. The darker the color, the greater the concentration of protein.

Mash samples of different foods separately in water. You might use flour, gelatin, pieces of potato, bread, milk, meat, crackers, and sugar. **Ask the adult** to help you test these foods for protein. Which foods give a positive test for protein? **Wash your hands after handling raw meat**.

2-7
Egg White Protein

With your parents' permission, remove three or four fresh eggs from the refrigerator and let them come to room temperature. Then separate the white from the yolk of an egg over a cereal bowl. If the yolk breaks and some becomes mixed with the egg white, set that bowl aside in the refrigerator. That egg can be used to make scrambled eggs later. Try again with another egg over another bowl. When you succeed in separating the egg white from an unbroken yolk, pour the egg white into a measuring cup. Then pour the egg white from the measuring cup into a test tube or a small glass. One egg white will probably provide a 5 cm (2 in) depth of liquid in the test tube. In a small glass, you may need two or three eggs to obtain a depth of 5 cm.

Things you will need:
- three or four fresh eggs at room temperature
- bowl
- measuring cup
- test tube or small glass
- ruler
- penlight or small flashlight
- electric or rotary hand mixer

Use a penlight or a small flashlight to test for the Tyndall effect (see Experiment 1-1 and Figure 1). What does this test tell you about the size of the molecules in egg white?

Pour some water into a glass or a test tube. Add a teaspoon of egg white and stir or shake. Does the egg white dissolve in water?

Use an electric or rotary hand mixer to churn the egg white until it becomes foamy. Does the foamy egg white dissolve in water? Has the physical beating of the egg white done anything to change its solubility in water? If it has, what, do you think, might have caused this change? **Wash your hands with soap and warm water after handling raw eggs**.

2-8*
Glue from Milk Protein

Milk contains a protein called casein. If you have ever seen sour milk, you have seen casein. It is the solid part of the sour milk. But you do not have to wait for milk to sour to separate casein molecules from milk. Adding acid to skim milk will have the same effect.

Pour a cup of skim milk into a pan. Add 2 tablespoons of white vinegar and place the pan on a stove. **Under adult supervision**, heat and stir the milk and vinegar until lumps (curds) begin to form. Remove the pan from the heat but keep stirring for as long as curds continue to form.

Things you will need:

- measuring cup
- skim milk
- cooking pan
- tablespoon
- white vinegar
- stove
- an adult
- strainer
- sink
- beaker or jar
- water
- teaspoon
- baking soda
- small sheets of paper

Next, pour the liquid and curds into a strainer over the sink. What kind of food do the curds in the strainer resemble? Empty the curds into a beaker or jar and add about 2 tablespoons of water and 1/2 teaspoon of baking soda to give them some body. Why do bubbles form in the mixture?

Once bubbling stops, spread some of the mixture over half a small sheet of paper. Place a second sheet on the first and press them together. After the mixture has had an hour or two to dry, try to pull the two sheets of paper apart. The protein works like glue.

Exploring on Your Own

Find out how cottage cheese is made.

When you were younger, you may have read about Little Miss Muffet who sat on a tuffet, eating some curds and whey. You know about curds, but what is whey? What is a tuffet?

Why is milk pasteurized?

What is homogenized milk?

How are cowpox and smallpox related?

2-9*
Glue from Gluten

Casein is only one of many proteins that can be used to make glue. As its name suggests, gluten, a protein found in flour, is the basis of another glue.

You can make some gluten-based glue by mixing hot water and flour. Pour 125 mL (1/2 cup) of water into a small pan. **Under adult supervision**, heat the water until it is about to boil. Then reduce the heat and add 60 mL (1/4 cup) of flour. Stir the flour and hot water over low heat until most of the lumps are gone and the mixture is uniform. Turn off the heat, let the mixture cool, and then pour it into a jar that has a lid. Place a small amount of the mixture in a paper cup and leave it exposed to the air.

Things you will need:
* graduated cylinder or measuring cup
* water
* small cooking pan
* an adult
* stove
* flour
* spoon
* jar with lid
* paper cup
* paper

Use a finger to spread some of the white glue over half a sheet of paper. Add a second sheet of paper and press the two together. After the glue has dried, try to pull the sheets apart. Here is another way to make white glue!

What happens to the glue in the paper cup after a day or two? Why should you keep the glue in a sealed jar?

Exploring on Your Own

You have prepared glue from gluten and from casein. Design an experiment to test the strength of each glue. Which glue is stronger? Can you change the strength of either glue by changing the proportions of the substances you mix in preparing the glues? Is either glue stronger if you add sugar to the mixture?

2-10
Charging Gelatin

Spread some unflavored gelatin powder over a small plate or saucer. Blow up a balloon and tie its neck. Then rub the balloon with a cloth or paper towel. Rubbing the balloon in this way will cause a static electric charge to collect on the balloon's sur-

Things you will need:

- unflavored gelatin powder
- small plate or saucer
- balloon
- cloth or paper towel
- flavored gelatin dessert powder

face. Slowly bring the balloon near the gelatin and listen carefully. What do you hear? What causes the sounds you hear? Look at the surface of the balloon closest to the gelatin. What has collected on the balloon? How can you explain its presence?

Again, move the balloon close to the gelatin. What causes "castles" to form in the gelatin? What evidence do you have to support the idea that there are charges in gelatin that can be induced to move by an external electric charge?

Repeat the experiment with a more colorful flavored gelatin dessert powder. Are the results the same?

2-11*
Gelatin: A Readily Available Protein

Flavored Gelatin Candy

Pour some unflavored gelatin powder into a medicine cup or a similar small container until it reaches a depth of about 3 cm (1 in). Use an eyedropper to add a drop of water to the center of the gelatin. What happens to the water? Continue to add water a drop at a time. Is gelatin capable of absorbing large amounts of water?

Repeat this experiment, using a flavored gelatin dessert powder. Add a drop of water to the center of the gelatin. After the eighth drop is absorbed, gently slide a fork under the center of the gelatin surface. Then, lift a candy treat from the flavored gelatin.

Things you will need:

- unflavored gelatin powder
- medicine cup or similar small container
- ruler
- eyedropper
- water
- flavored gelatin dessert powder
- fork
- measuring cup
- teakettle
- spoons
- small glass or test tube
- dark room or hallway
- penlight or small flashlight
- coffee filter
- funnel
- refrigerator
- pan of hot water

Gelatin: Sols and Gels

Pour a package of unflavored gelatin into 125 mL (1/2 cup) of cold water. Stir the mixture. Does gelatin dissolve in cold water?

Pour the 125 mL of water and gelatin into a bowl. Then add 375 mL (1 1/2 cups) of boiling water to the bowl. Stir the mixture. Does the gelatin dissolve in the hot water?

Between true solutions and mixtures, in which particles separate into distinct phases, as happens with precipitates and emulsions, there are colloids. The particles that make up a colloid are so small that they cannot be seen even with a microscope, and they cannot be separated by filtering. However, the particles are large enough to scatter light, so they exhibit the Tyndall effect. In fact, careful analysis of the way the light scatters can be used to determine much about the size and shape of the molecules of the solid.

Colloids are classified as sols, emulsions, aerosols, and gels. In a sol, large particles of solid are spread evenly through a liquid. In emulsions, tiny particles of one liquid are spread uniformly through another liquid. For example, in homogenized milk, cream is broken up into particles so small that they remain dispersed through the watery part of the milk. Aerosols can be either smokes or fogs. A smoke is a dispersion of tiny solid particles throughout a gas; in a fog, liquid is dispersed through the gas. A smog is a combination of smoke and fog. Finally, a gel is an unusual type of colloid in which a liquid is dispersed uniformly through a solid. Sols may sometimes become gels when cooled.

Pour some of the gelatin mixture, which is a sol, into a small glass or test tube. Take it into a dark room or hallway and shine a penlight or small flashlight into the sol. Is there a Tyndall effect? What does this tell you about the size of the dissolved particles of gelatin? Do the gelatin particles slowly settle out of the water as a precipitate, or do they remain spread uniformly throughout the water? Fold a coffee filter and place it in a funnel. Place the funnel in another glass or test tube. Pour the mixture of water and gelatin through the filter. Does filtering separate the gelatin from the water?

The gelatin protein that you mixed with hot water is a sol by definition. Can it be changed to a gel?

After the sol has cooled, place it, both the glass or test tube and the bowl of it, in a refrigerator, where it will cool well below room temperature. After several hours, look at the gelatin. What has happened to the sol? What would you call it now?

Shine a narrow beam of light into the glass or test tube containing the gel. Is there a Tyndall effect?

Can you convert the gel back to a sol? Try it by putting the glass or tube of gel into a pan of hot water. Does the gel return to its sol state?

Exploring on Your Own

Ask your parent or guardian for permission to prepare a flavored gelatin dessert. **With adult supervision,** follow the directions on the package. When the gelatin has cooled and is ready to eat, use a spoon to remove some of it and place it on a small plate. Then use a knife to cut it into cubes about 3 cm (1 in) on a side. Leave the cubes on a small plate in the refrigerator. Each day eat one of the cubes. What do you notice about the nature of the gel as time passes? Does it become drier? Does liquid seem to be escaping from the solid?

3

Kitchen Liquids

Your kitchen contains a great variety of liquids. Some of them are acids, some are bases, some are neither. Some are thick, some are thin, some are heavy, some are light. In this chapter, you will learn how to identify acids and bases, using indicators that you can prepare from materials commonly found in kitchens. You will also build a battery that will clean silver; carry out experiments to find out how the poles (+ or –) of a battery can be identified; find ways to measure a liquid's thickness (viscosity); determine how thickness is affected by temperature; and decide whether or not a liquid's thickness is related to its heaviness (density).

Acids and Bases in the Kitchen

Two types of chemicals found in the kitchen are acids and bases. *Acid* comes from the Latin word *acidus*, meaning "sharp" or "sour." That is how sour-tasting foods and chemicals came to be known as acids. In addition to their sour taste, acids dissolve in water to form solutions that conduct electricity; they contain hydrogen that is released when the acid is added to certain metals such as zinc; they turn blue litmus red; and they neutralize bases: that is, they combine with a base to form a substance that is neither an acid nor a base. Substances that are neither acidic nor basic, such as water, are said to be neutral.

Bases are also called *alkalies*, a word that means "ashes." Long before there were chemists there were ashes, the remains of wood after it is burned. Ashes have the properties that chemists use to identify alkaline substances, or bases. Bases have a bitter taste and feel slippery like soap. Early American settlers made soap by boiling animal fat with wood ashes that had been washed. Bases, like acids, are conductors of electricity, but they turn red litmus blue, have a bitter taste, and neutralize acids.

Acids and bases conduct electricity because they form charged atoms, called ions, when they dissolve in water. Acids form hydrogen ions (H^+), and bases form hydroxide ions (OH^-). This chemical equation should help you understand how acids and bases neutralize each other to form water (HOH, or H_2O):

$$H^+ + OH^- \rightarrow HOH, \text{ or } H_2O$$

3-1*
Identifying Acids and Bases in the Kitchen

Place a drop of lemon juice on your tongue. Do you think lemon juice is an acid or a base? Why?

To test your hypothesis, you might dip pieces of red and blue litmus into the liquid. However, since we are dealing with kitchen foods and chemicals, you can make your own acid-base indicator.

Remove a few leaves from a red cabbage. Break the leaves into small pieces and put them in a nonaluminum cooking pot. Cover the leaves with water and, **under adult supervision**, put the pot on the stove. When the water begins to boil, cover the pan and turn down the heat so that the water boils quietly. After about 20 minutes, remove the pot from the stove and let it cool.

When the pot is cool, use forceps or tongs to remove the cabbage leaves. Pour the water and cabbage juice extracted from the leaves into a jar. Store it in the refrigerator until you are ready to use it.

Things you will need:

- lemon juice
- red cabbage
- nonaluminum pot and cover
- stove
- an adult
- water
- clock
- forceps or tongs
- jar
- refrigerator
- eyedropper
- vinegar
- clear household ammonia
- apple juice, grapefruit juice, and orange juice
- milk
- cleansing powder
- rubbing alcohol
- salt and sugar
- aspirin
- wood ashes
- baking soda and baking powder
- limewater
- Kool-Aid crystals
- Tang crystals
- olive jar juice
- pickle juice
- ginger ale
- tonic water
- seltzer water
- pen or pencil and paper

The color of cabbage juice, like the color of litmus, is affected by acids and bases. The purplish cabbage juice that you have prepared will turn a pinkish red in an acid and green in a base. It is a more sensitive indicator than litmus because in a very weak base—one that forms few hydroxide ions in water—it will have a bluish tint. In a weak acid—one that forms few hydrogen ions—the pinkish red is less intense.

You can use your cabbage juice indicator to test a number of kitchen foods and chemicals to see whether they are acidic, basic, or neutral. For solid substances, you should add water to make a small amount of solution before adding a drop of the cabbage juice indicator. In addition to lemon juice, you might try vinegar, clear household ammonia, apple juice, grapefruit juice, orange juice, milk, cleansing powder, rubbing alcohol, salt, sugar, aspirin, wood ashes, baking soda, baking powder, limewater, Kool-Aid crystals, Tang crystals, the juice from an olive jar, pickle juice, ginger ale, tonic water, and seltzer water. You can make limewater by obtaining lime from a garden supply store. Stir one teaspoon of the white solid into a small jar of water. Put a lid on the jar and let the mixture settle overnight. Carefully pour the liquid into a second jar, leaving any white solid behind.

Make a chart with three columns. Label one column *acids*, another *bases*, and a third *neutral*. On the basis of the color you saw when cabbage juice was added, place the names of the substances you tested in the proper column.

Exploring on Your Own

During Experiment 1-5, you were asked to save the white solid (magnesium hydroxide) that you collected. Place some of the solid in a small jar or test tube and add a few milliliters of water. Save the rest for Experiment 3-2.

Test the mixture of magnesium hydroxide and water with cabbage juice. Is it acidic, basic, or neutral?

Vitamin C, as you know, is ascorbic acid. Crush a vitamin C tablet into a powder and add some water. Predict the color of the cabbage juice indicator after it is added to the vitamin C solution. Were you right?

You have seen that cabbage juice is an acid-base indicator. Test a number of other fruits and vegetables to see if you can find other natural acid-base indicators.

3-2*
Another Natural Indicator

Add some lemon juice to a cup of hot tea. What evidence do you have that tea is an acid-base indicator? There are many natural acid-base indicators. You have used red cabbage juice, now try unsweetened red grape juice. Add a few drops of the grape juice to several milliliters of white vinegar in a small glass jar or test tube. What is the color of the grape juice in an acid? Add a few drops of the grape juice to a few milliliters of ammonia solution. What is the color of the grape juice in a base?

Add a few drops of grape juice to some tap water. What is the color of the grape juice indicator in a neutral solution? Why is cabbage juice a better indicator than grape juice?

Based on the tests you did in the previous experiment, predict the color of unsweetened grape juice in each of the substances you tried before. Then test your predictions experimentally.

Things you will need:

- lemon juice
- hot tea
- unsweetened red grape juice
- eyedropper
- white vinegar
- small glass jar or test tube
- clear household ammonia
- water
- apple juice, grapefruit juice, and orange juice
- milk
- cleansing powder
- rubbing alcohol
- salt and sugar
- aspirin
- wood ashes
- baking soda and baking powder
- limewater
- Kool-Aid crystals
- Tang crystals
- olive jar juice
- pickle juice
- ginger ale
- tonic water and seltzer water
- pen or pencil and paper

Exploring on Your Own

You can use what you have learned about acid-base indicators and neutralization to carry out what will look like magic to your friends and family. To prepare for your show, dilute 20 mL (2/3 oz.) of unsweetened red grape juice with 180 mL (6 oz.) of water to reduce the intensity of the color. Pour the diluted juice into a glass. In a second glass, place a few drops of ammonia solution. When you pour the grape juice into the second glass, it will turn green because ammonia is a base. In a third glass, place more than enough vinegar to neutralize the base. (You will need to practice to get the right amounts of ammonia and vinegar.) When you pour the green liquid into the third glass, it turns back to a red liquid because the excess vinegar makes the liquid acidic again. **Do not put anything with ammonia in it near or in your mouth.**

Tell your friends and family that you can change red liquid to green liquid and then back to red again. Then proceed to use the chemicals you have prepared to carry out your "magic."

Do some research to add more chemical "magic" until you have a show that you can use to entertain friends, classmates, and students in lower grades.

3-3
Acid + Base = Neutral Substance

One characteristic of acids and bases is their ability to neutralize each other. To see how an acid and a base combine to form a neutral substance, pour about 10 mL (2 teaspoons) of vinegar into a small jar or beaker. Add a few drops of red cabbage juice. Stir the mixture until it has a uniform color. Rinse the eye-

Things you will need:

- white vinegar
- teaspoon or graduated cylinder
- small jar or beaker
- red cabbage juice
- eyedropper
- spoon or other stirring device
- clear household ammonia
- baking soda

dropper, then use it to add clear household ammonia drop by drop to the vinegar. Look carefully to see what happens to the color of the solution around the area where the ammonia drops land. Now stir the liquid as you add the drops until you see a distinct color change. What has happened?

Rinse the eyedropper again, then use it to add drops of vinegar to the basic solution. Do this a drop at a time. Notice the effect of one drop on the color of the solution. Look for an intermediate purple color (the color of cabbage juice in neutral water) just before the solution changes from acid to base or base to acid. When you see the indicator turn purple, the solution is neutral.

What happens to the color of the neutral solution if you add a drop or two of vinegar? A drop or two of ammonia?

A drop or two of an acid can turn a neutral solution acidic. But suppose you have something that reacts with the acid. What will happen then? To find out, add some water to a teaspoonful of baking soda in a small jar or beaker. Add a few drops of the indicator to the baking soda. Now slowly add vinegar to the solution. Once you reach the neutralization point, is the color change from neutral to acidic sudden or gradual? Can you explain why?

3-4
Acidic Foods and Apples

You have probably seen what happens to apple slices when they are exposed to air. The oxygen in the air reacts with the apple to form a brown layer. To see how this reaction can be prevented, cut three flat slices from an apple and put them on a plate. Spread some Kool-Aid or Tang crystals (acid) on one piece. Crush a vitamin C tablet (ascorbic acid) and spread it on the second slice. Leave the third slice exposed to the air as a control. Watch these pieces over a 24-hour period. What effect do the acids have on the browning of apples in air? What effect would lemon juice have on the browning of an apple slice? Test an apple slice with lemon juice. Was your prediction correct? Why do you think apples in a fruit salad that contains grapefruit, oranges, or other citrus fruits do not turn brown?

Things you will need:

• apple
• knife
• plate
• Kool-Aid or Tang crystals
• vitamin C tablet
• lemon juice

3-5
Acids, Bases, and Conductivity

Another characteristic of acids and bases is their conductivity, which is the result of the ions they form in water. For example, vinegar, which is a solution of acetic acid ($C_2H_4O_2$), forms hydrogen ions (H^+) and acetate ions ($C_2H_3O_2^-$) in water. A base such as ammonia solution forms hydroxide ions (OH^-) and ammonium ions (NH_4^+) in water. Because acids and bases form ions in water, their solutions contain charged particles that can move, creating an electric current (a flow of charge).

The acids you have used in this chapter, such as vinegar and lemon juice, are weak acids. Strong acids, such as sulfuric, hydrochloric, and nitric acids, form large numbers of hydrogen ions in water and are more dangerous to work with because they can damage flesh. Weak acids do not form nearly as many ions; consequently, they do not conduct electricity nearly as well as strong acids. Similarly, weak bases, such as ammonia, produce far fewer hydroxide ions than do strong and more dangerous bases, such as sodium hydroxide (NaOH). Nevertheless, weak acids and bases should carry a small current when connected to a battery. Batteries use chemical reactions to produce electric current.

You can build an inexpensive device like the one in Figure 12 to test liquids for conductivity. Make a current detector by wrapping 50 turns of enameled copper magnet wire around a magnetic

Things you will need:

- enameled copper magnet wire
- magnetic compass
- sandpaper
- ruler
- masking tape
- 3 insulated wires with alligator clips
- 6-volt lantern battery
- two large paper clips
- plastic vial
- liquids that were acids or bases when tested with red cabbage juice in Experiment 3-1
- tap water
- distilled water
- salt solution

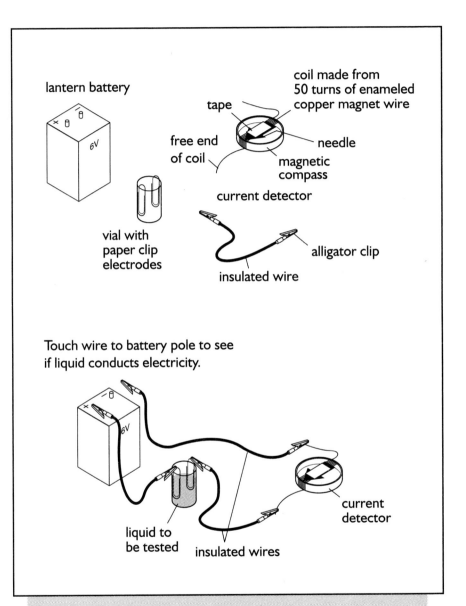

lantern battery

coil made from
50 turns of enameled
copper magnet wire

tape

free end
of coil

needle

magnetic
compass

current detector

6V

vial with
paper clip
electrodes

alligator clip

insulated wire

Touch wire to battery pole to see
if liquid conducts electricity.

6V

current
detector

liquid to
be tested

insulated wires

Figure 12. A current detector, battery, wires, and a vial with paper clip electrodes
can be used to test liquid for conductivity.

compass. The enamel serves to insulate the wire. Leave about 15 cm (6 in) of wire at each end of the coil for connecting lead wires to the battery. Use a small piece of sandpaper to remove the insulating enamel from the last 3 cm (1 in) of each end of the coil. The coils, which can be held together with small pieces of masking tape, should be parallel to the compass needle.

To see how the detector works, connect each end of the coil to an insulated wire. Connect one wire to one pole of the battery. Then momentarily touch the other wire to the other pole of the battery. What happens to the compass needle when electricity flows through the coil that surrounds it?

Put two large paper clips on opposite sides of a plastic vial. Use insulated wires with alligator clips to connect one paper clip to a pole of a lantern battery and the other paper clip to a lead of the current detector. Clip the other insulated wire to the current detector. Leave the other end of this wire free.

In Experiment 3-1, you tested various liquids with red cabbage juice. Now you can take those liquids that your indicator revealed to be acids or bases and test them for conductivity. Fill the vial with one of the liquids you believe to be an acid or a base. The paper clips will serve as electrodes, and the liquid will become part of the circuit shown in Figure 12. Touch the free wire to the pole of the battery that is not already connected. What happens to the compass needle? Try other liquids that were acids or bases according to the red cabbage juice indicator. Are they conductors?

Compare the deflection of the compass needle that you find for liquids you believe to be acids or bases with the deflection you obtain with tap water. Does tap water contain any ions? How about distilled water?

Because salt is made up of ions, a salt solution contains many more charged particles than a weak acid or base. To compare the conductivity of a salt solution with the weak acids and bases you found in your kitchen, pour some salt solution into the vial and test for conductivity. How does the deflection of the compass needle compare with the deflection you obtained for a weak acid or a weak base?

Test some other substances to see whether they will conduct electricity. Do you think a sugar solution will conduct electricity? How about cooking oil? Alcohol? Egg white? Test your predictions. Were you correct?

3-6*
A Potato as a Battery Pole Indicator

In the previous experiment, it did not matter to which battery pole the ends of the wire coil were connected, as long as they were connected to opposite poles. However, in experiments where the direction of the current flow is important, one needs to know

whether a wire lead is connected to the positive or negative pole of the battery. Usually, the poles are marked with a + or a −, but if they are not, or if the marks have been rubbed off, you can still identify the poles. All you need is a freshly cut potato, two insulated wires with alligator clips, and two pieces of copper. You can use copper nails, short lengths of heavy copper wire, or two copper pennies.

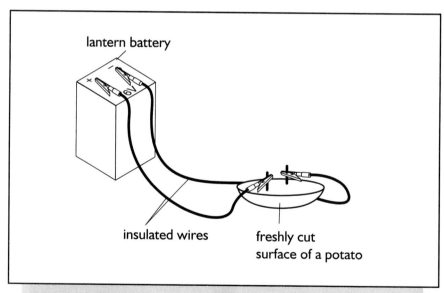

lantern battery

insulated wires

freshly cut surface of a potato

Figure 13. A potato and copper electrodes can be used to identify the poles of a battery.

Push the pieces of copper into the freshly cut surface of a potato, as shown in Figure 13. The two pieces of copper will serve as electrodes for the potato, which contains charged particles. Because the flesh of a potato contains charged particles, it can conduct charge just as acids, bases, and salt solutions can. Connect two wires to the copper electrodes and to the poles of a 6-volt lantern battery that are identified as + and –. Wait a few minutes. Around which electrode does a greenish color appear? Is this electrode connected to the positive or negative pole of the battery? (You may be able to see small bubbles of hydrogen being released at the other electrode.) How can a potato be used to identify the pole of a battery?

Exploring on Your Own

Do some research to determine why a greenish color appears around one electrode, while bubbles of hydrogen form at the other electrode. Hints: What is the color of many copper salts when dissolved in water? What is the metal in the magnet wire?

3-7*
Gases, Liquids, and Diffusion

In earlier experiments you saw that a solution made by dissolving ammonia in water is a base. If you open a bottle of household ammonia, you will soon smell some of the ammonia gas that comes out of the solution

Things you will need:

• solution of household ammonia
• a friend
• clock or watch with a second hand

because the gas diffuses (spreads) through the air. **Do not sniff ammonia directly**.

According to the atomic-molecular theory, molecules are in constant motion. It is the motion of ammonia molecules that enables them to travel from a bottle to your nose. The mathematics of the theory makes it possible to predict the average speed of ammonia molecules at any given temperature. Ammonia molecules at room temperature have an average speed of approximately 660 meters per second (m/s), or 1,500 miles per hour.

Have a friend open a bottle of household ammonia on one side of a room while you stand on the other side where you can view a clock or your watch. How long does it take before you can smell the ammonia?

Exploring on Your Own

If molecules of ammonia move at an average speed of 660 m/s, why does it take so long for them to diffuse through the air in the room? Could it be related to the fact that there are approximately 25 quintillion (25,000,000,000,000,000,000) molecules in each cubic centimeter of air?

The atomic-molecular theory also indicates that the average speed of molecules is related to their temperature. If this is true, should a drop of food coloring diffuse faster in hot water or in cold water? Design an experiment to find out.

3-8*
A Silver-Cleaning Battery

You can make a battery that will clean silverware without the elbow grease required with a liquid cleaner. Batteries have two electrodes. A conducting material called the electrolyte lies between the electrodes. In this battery, the silver acts as the positive electrode of the battery. The purpose of this battery is not to provide an electric current to light a bulb or turn a motor. This battery's function is to make use of the chemical reaction that produces electric charge to clean its silver electrode.

Things you will need:
- large cooking pan
- heavy-duty aluminum foil
- measuring cup
- teaspoon
- stove
- hot water
- tarnished silverware
- salt
- baking soda
- an adult
- forceps or tongs
- sink

To make such a battery, find a cooking pan large enough to hold the tarnished piece or pieces of silver. A deep frying pan may serve the purpose. Line the inside of the pan with heavy-duty aluminum foil. The aluminum will serve as the negative pole (electrode) of the battery. Place the tarnished silverware on the aluminum. Be sure each piece touches the foil.

Use a measuring cup to add hot water to the pan. Add enough to cover the silverware; however, the pan should not be full, because you are going to boil the water. For every liter or quart of water you pour into the pan, add a teaspoon of salt and a teaspoon of baking soda. These substances provide a solution that will act as the battery's electrolyte.

Under adult supervision, heat the pan on a stove until the solution begins to boil. Then lower the heat so that the liquid boils quietly. The silver sulfide tarnish dissolves slowly, providing silver ions (Ag$^+$) and sulfide ions (S^{--}) to the solution. Negatively charged electrons are transferred from the aluminum atoms (Al) to the silver ions (Ag+). The result is formation of aluminum ions (Al^{+++}) and neutral silver atoms (Ag). The silver atoms collect on the silverware, which is the positive pole of the battery. The sulfide ions unite with various positive ions in the solution to form the insoluble sulfides seen on the foil.

After the tarnish has been transferred from the silver to the aluminum foil, turn off the heat. Use forceps or tongs to remove the silverware from the pan. Place it in a sink where it can be washed and rinsed. Dry the silverware and return it to wherever it is stored. When the pan has cooled, pour the solution into the sink and discard the aluminum foil.

Exploring on Your Own

At the library, investigate how different batteries work. What is common to all batteries? How do batteries differ? What is the difference between a battery and an electric cell?

Under adult supervision, build a simple battery and show that it can be used to light a flashlight bulb or turn a small electric motor.

Liquids and Their Viscosity or Thickness

If you drag a box across the floor, a force called friction opposes the motion. The force depends on the weight of the box, the materials of which it is made, and the kind of floor over which it slides. Friction also results when a fluid such as water or air flows through a pipe. There is friction between the layer of water or air in contact with the pipe. There are also frictional forces within the liquid itself. This can be demonstrated with a wooden and a cardboard disk like those shown in Figure 14. If the wooden disk is made to spin at high speed by means of a pulley connected by a belt to a motor, the cardboard disk hanging freely from above will begin to rotate in the same direction and gradually increase in speed.

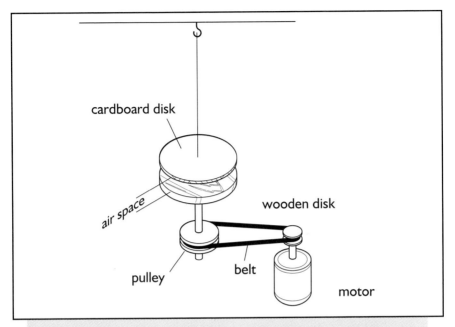

cardboard disk

air space

wooden disk

pulley

belt

motor

Figure 14. When the wooden disk rotates, the cardboard disk will begin to turn in the same direction, despite the fact that there is only air between the two disks.

Since the only connection between the two disks is air, it must be the frictional forces between the molecules of air as well as between the air and the disks that cause the cardboard disk to move. If the same experiment is performed in a vacuum (where there is no air), the cardboard disk does not move.

Do these frictional forces within liquids, which are called viscous forces, vary with different kinds of liquids? To find out, you can measure the time it takes for different liquids to pass through a narrow opening or for a marble to fall through a narrow tube filled with different liquids.

3-9
Kitchen Liquids Thick and Thin

For this experiment, you will need a tall, cylindrical, transparent, narrow tube closed at one end and a marble with a diameter slightly smaller than the tube's diameter. The marble should fit into the tube but with very little space between it and the tube's wall. The longer the tube and the closer the fit, the better. You probably have some marbles of various sizes. If you do not have a tube such as the one described, you can probably find one in a variety store. They are sometimes used as packaging for long thin objects or candy. Another source is your school's science department. It may have such tubing. If not, it probably has large test tubes.

Things you will need:

- tall, cylindrical, transparent, narrow tube closed at one end (200 mm [8 in] x 25 mm [1 in] test tube works well)
- marble with a diameter slightly smaller than the tube's diameter
- cold tap water
- a partner
- stopwatch or watch with a second hand
- paper and pencil
- various liquids such as soapy water, alcohol, saturated salt and sugar solutions, cooking oil, syrup, and molasses
- beaker or measuring cup
- soap
- hot water
- towel

Standard test tubes that are 200 mm (8 in) long with a diameter of 25 mm (1 in) work well.

You might begin this experiment using cold tap water from the kitchen sink. Fill the tube with water. Hold the marble so that it is just touching the liquid, as shown in Figure 15. Have a partner with a stopwatch or a watch with a second hand or mode say "go." At the moment you hear the word "go," release the marble. When the marble reaches the bottom of the tube, say "stop!" When your partner hears you say "stop," he or she will stop the stopwatch or note the position of the second hand on the watch.

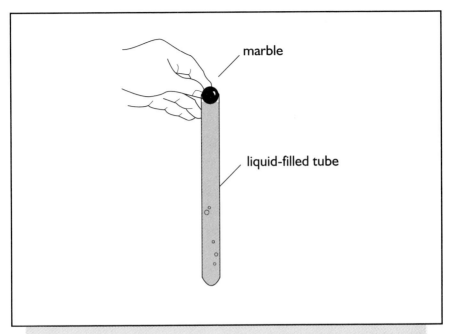

Figure 15. How fast will a marble fall through a tube filled with a liquid? Does its rate of fall depend on the kind of liquid in the tube?

Record the time it took the marble to fall through the column of water. Then repeat the experiment several times to be sure your results are consistent. Find the average time for the marble to fall to the bottom of the tube. How does the time for the marble to fall through water compare with the time to fall through an equal length of air?

Repeat the experiment, using different liquids. You might try soapy water, alcohol, saturated salt and sugar solutions, cooking oil, syrup, molasses, and a one-to-one mixture of molasses and water. You will also need a beaker or measuring cup into which you can pour the liquid, retrieve the marble, and pour the liquid back into the tube so that you can make several runs and obtain an average time. After using each liquid, wash the tube and marble with warm soapy water, rinse with hot water, and dry with a towel.

You have been testing the viscosity of liquids. Viscosity is the resistance of a liquid to flow due to friction within the liquid. Based on your findings, which liquid do you think is the most viscous? Which liquid is the least viscous? List the liquids you used in order of their viscosity. Which of the liquids you tested would you call thick based on the way they feel? Which liquids would you call thin? Does a liquid's viscosity seem to be related to what you may call thickness? If so, how are they related?

3-10
Kitchen Liquids, Viscosity, and Temperature

You have probably heard the expression, As slow as molasses. From the results of your previous experiment, you can understand the origin of that saying. You may also have heard someone say, As slow as molasses in January. The second saying would suggest a relationship between temperature and viscosity. To see whether there is such a relationship, you can repeat Experiment 3-9, using liquids at different temperatures.

Place cooking oil, syrup, and molasses (enough of each to more than fill the tube) in a refrigerator to cool. Place a thermometer inside the refrigerator so that you will know its internal temperature. While these liquids are cooling, prepare some ice water in a glass. Stir the ice and water until the temperature of the water is very close to its

Things you will need:

- tall, cylindrical, transparent, narrow tube closed at one end (200 mm [8 in] x 25 mm [1 in] test tube works well)

- marble with a diameter slightly smaller than the tube's diameter

- cold tap water

- a partner

- stopwatch or watch with a second hand

- paper and pencil

- various liquids such as soapy water, alcohol, saturated salt and sugar solutions, cooking oil, syrup, and molasses

- beaker or measuring cup

- soap

- hot water

- towel

- refrigerator

- thermometer (-10–110°C)

- ice

- glass

freezing point (0°C). Pour the ice water into the tube you used in Experiment 3-9 and, with your partner, measure and record the time it takes for the marble to descend through it. Repeat several times with fresh samples of ice water. What is the average time for the marble to fall through the ice water?

Repeat the experiment, using hot tap water, noting the water's temperature. What is the average time for the marble to fall through the hot water? Does temperature have any effect on the viscous nature of water? If it does, how?

When the liquids that are cooling reach the same temperature as the air inside the refrigerator, you can begin testing them. First, repeat the experiment in which you let a marble fall through cooking oil at room temperature. What do you find is the average time for the marble to descend through the cooking oil? Does it agree quite closely with your results in the previous experiment?

Now pour cold cooking oil into the tube and measure the time for the marble to fall. How does temperature affect the viscosity of cooking oil?

Try to predict how temperature will affect the viscosity of syrup and molasses. Carry out the experiments to see whether your predictions are correct. Are they? How do you think temperature will affect the viscosity of a one-to-one mixture of molasses and water?

3-11*
Pouring Speed, Viscosity, and Temperature

Another way to compare the viscous nature of different liquids is to measure the time it takes for them to empty from a container. You can use a clean can such as a soup can to hold the liquid. **Ask an adult** to drill a hole through the center of the bottom of the can, using a 3-mm (1/8-in) bit. Alternatively, you can use a nail to make a hole of similar size through the bottom of a Styrofoam cup.

Place your finger over the hole in the bottom of the container. Using tap water at room temperature, fill the can to a convenient level that you can identify. When you are ready to

Things you will need:

- clean metal can such as a soup can, or Styrofoam cup
- soap and water
- an adult
- drill and a 3-mm (1/8-in) bit or a small nail
- tap water
- thermometer
- stopwatch or watch with a second hand
- a partner
- pencil and paper
- cooking oil
- clean container
- syrup
- molasses

begin the experiment, have a partner with a stopwatch or a watch with a second hand say "go!" At that moment, remove your finger. The water will flow from the can in a steady stream. At the moment the steady stream stops and the water begins to drip from the can, say "stop!" Your partner will note the time that elapsed while the can emptied. Record the time and repeat the experiment several times to be sure your results are reasonably consistent. Then record the average time for water to empty from the can based on all the runs you made.

Repeat the experiment, using cooking oil at room temperature. In this case, you will want to let the oil empty into another clean container so that it can be reused. As compared with water, do you think it will take cooking oil more or less time to empty from the can? Was your prediction correct?

How will the emptying times for syrup and molasses compare with those for water and cooking oil? Measure the emptying times for these liquids. (Again, you should let these liquids empty into another clean container so that they can be reused.) Were your predictions correct?

Exploring on Your Own

If you fill the can with water to half the height you used before, will it take half as long to empty? Try it! Can you explain your results?

Ask an adult to double the size of the hole in the can by using a 6-mm (1/4-in) bit. How do you think doubling the diameter of the hole will affect the emptying time? Will it halve the time because the hole is twice as wide, or will it quarter the time because the hole's area is now four times as great?

Carry out experiments to find the relationship between the size of the hole in the bottom of the can and the time for the can to empty. Write an equation for this relationship. Can you explain the relationship?

3-12
Viscosity and Density

Perhaps the viscosity, or thickness, of a substance is related to its density, or heaviness. People often refer to a substance as being heavy when they mean that it is dense; that is, its mass per volume is large when compared with other substances. For example, we often say lead is heavy, but a kilogram of lead has

Things you will need:

• graduated cylinder or measuring cup

• balance or scale

• water

• cooking oil

• molasses

• soap and warm water to clean vessels

the same mass as a kilogram of water or anything else. What we should say is that lead is denser than, say, water or iron. A kilogram of lead occupies a volume of only 88 cubic centimeters (cm^3), so it is more compact (denser) than a kilogram of iron, which has a volume of 127 cm^3, or a kilogram of water, which fills an entire liter (1,000 cm^3). Air is even less dense. A kilogram of air occupies more than 800 liters, or 800,000 cm^3.

It might be reasonable to think that a marble falls more slowly through cooking oil than through water because the cooking oil is denser as well as thicker and, therefore, provides more buoyancy to the marble than does water. To see whether the viscosity of different substances really is related to their density, you can weigh equal volumes of the various liquids you used in comparing viscosities.

You will need a graduated cylinder or measuring cup and a balance or scale. A convenient volume to use is 100 cm^3, or 100 milliliters (mL). (100 cm^3 and 100 mL are the same volume because 1 cm^3 = 1 mL.)

Weigh the graduated cylinder first. Then fill it to the 100-mL line with water. Be sure the *bottom* of the meniscus (the curved surface of the liquid) is on the line, as shown in Figure 16. What is the mass of 100 mL of water? What is the mass of 100 mL of cooking

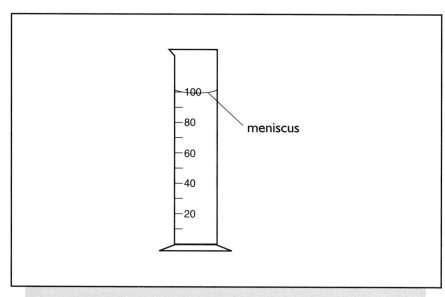

Figure 16. Because water adheres to glass, the water touching the glass is higher than the rest of the liquid's surface. This makes the water's surface curve, forming a meniscus.

oil? Of 100 mL of molasses? Of a one-to-one mixture of water and molasses? Of other liquids whose volumes and masses you may want to measure? What is the density (mass ÷ volume) of water? Of cooking oil? Of molasses? Of a one-to-one mixture of molasses and water? Of other liquids?

Based on your results, is the viscosity (thickness) of a substance related to its density? What evidence do you have to support your answer?

4

Baking Chemistry

In this chapter you will learn why yeast is the baker's favorite organism and how that organism reacts with sugars. Most bread is made with a leavening agent, such as yeast, that causes fermentation (a change in form) and the production of carbon dioxide. (The word *leaven* comes from the Latin word *levare*, which means "to raise.") The empty spaces you find in bread make it light and fluffy. Those empty spaces were filled with carbon dioxide when the bread was baking.

Before the Egyptians discovered a way to make leavened bread about 4,500 years ago, all bread was heavier because it was unleavened. Unleavened bread is still made and is used in the Jewish festival of Passover.

You will also find out why baking soda or baking powder, which contains acid in a solid form, can replace yeast as a leavening agent in many recipes. You will discover, too, that baking soda has a myriad of uses, many of which often have nothing to do with baking.

4–1*
Yeast: The Baker's and Brewer's Favorite Organisms

Yeasts are one-celled fungi. Like all fungi, they have no chlorophyll and, therefore, cannot manufacture their own food. Instead, they must absorb and digest organic matter. One commercially important food source for yeast is sugar. Yeasts are able to obtain their energy by converting sugar to alcohol and carbon dioxide. The chemical equation below represents this process. It shows that a sugar molecule consisting of 6 carbon atoms combined with 12 hydrogen atoms and 6 oxygen atoms, in the presence of yeast, is converted to 2 molecules of ethyl alcohol (C_2H_6O) and 2 molecules of carbon dioxide (CO_2).

$$C_6H_{12}O_6 + \text{yeast} \rightarrow 2C_2H_6O + 2CO_2$$

Alcohol is the product sought by brewers, and carbon dioxide is the product that bakers use to make bread and other baked goods rise.

Glucose ($C_6H_{12}O_6$) is often obtained from sucrose ($C_{12}H_{22}O_{11}$)—the white solid we use to sweeten our tea and cereal.

Things you will need:

- masking tape
- marking pen
- one or more muffin tins
- granulated sugar
- syrup
- powdered sugar
- brown sugar
- diet sweetener
- flour
- cornstarch
- raw hamburger
- salt
- cooking oil
- milk
- dry yeast
- water
- tablespoon
- measuring cup
- teaspoon
- toothpicks
- paper and pen or pencil
- an adult
- oven
- clock or watch

Sucrose can be converted to glucose by enzymes in the cells of yeast (and by enzymes in our own stomachs).

The carbon dioxide produced when yeast acts on sugar can be detected by the bubbles formed as carbon dioxide gas is released in the reaction. You can use the carbon dioxide bubbles to compare the effect of yeast on different foods.

To do this, first use masking tape and a marking pen to place the following labels next to the cups in one or more muffin tins: *control, granulated sugar, syrup, powdered sugar, brown sugar, diet sweetener, flour, cornstarch, raw hamburger, salt, cooking oil,* and *milk.* **Be sure to wash your hands with soap and warm water if you touch the raw meat.** Next, prepare a mixture of yeast and water by adding a tablespoon of dry yeast to a measuring cup that contains 250 mL (1 cup) of warm (35°C, or 95°F) water. Stir the mixture until it is uniform. Then add a tablespoon of this mixture to each of the 12 labeled muffin tin cups.

To the cup labeled *Control,* add nothing more. It will serve as the control in this experiment. To the yeast-water mixture in the other 11 cups, add, as labeled, 1/4 teaspoon of one of the following: granulated sugar (sucrose), pancake syrup, powdered sugar (sucrose), brown sugar, diet sweetener, flour, cornstarch, raw hamburger, salt, cooking oil, and milk. Stir the contents of each cup with a toothpick. In which ones do you see bubbles right away? Record your observations.

Under adult supervision, put the tin or tins in a warm (50°C, or 120°F) oven for about 10–15 minutes. Then check to see which samples show evidence of carbon dioxide bubbles. Place the tin(s) back in the warm oven and check for bubbles again after another 10–15 minutes. Record your observations each time. Does time have any effect on the production of carbon dioxide from the warm yeast-water-food mixtures? Which food or foods produced the most carbon dioxide when mixed with yeast and water?

91

What effect does the concentration of sugar have on the production of carbon dioxide? To find out, place a tablespoon of the yeast-water mixture in each of 5 muffin tin cups. Add 1/4 teaspoon of sugar to the first cup, 1/2 teaspoon to the second, 1 teaspoon to the third, and 2 teaspoons to the fourth. Add no sugar to the fifth cup; it will serve as a control. Label the cups, and put the muffin tin in a warm place. How does the concentration of sugar affect the production of carbon dioxide?

Exploring on Your Own

Design an experiment to find out how temperature affects the production of yeast from a yeast-water-sugar mixture. You can obtain a variety of temperatures by using a freezer, a refrigerator, a heated room, and an oven. What temperature provides the greatest production of carbon dioxide? What is the effect of extreme temperatures on the production of carbon dioxide? How can you explain this temperature effect?

To see that the gas produced from the sugar-water-yeast mixture really is carbon dioxide, you can test it with limewater. Limewater turns milky in the presence of carbon dioxide. If you do not have any limewater, you can make some by obtaining lime from a garden or agricultural supply store. Just stir a teaspoon of the white solid into a small jar of water. Put a lid on the jar and let the mixture settle overnight. Carefully pour the liquid into a second jar, leaving any white solid behind. Then screw the lid on the jar.

To see the effect of carbon dioxide (CO_2) on limewater, pour a small volume of limewater into a clear vial. Then use a drinking straw to blow your lung air, which is about 4 percent CO_2, gently into the limewater. What happens to the limewater? **Do not drink the limewater**.

Prepare another yeast-water-sugar mixture by adding 1/2 teaspoon of yeast and an equal amount of sugar to a measuring cup that contains 50 mL of warm water (35°C, or 95°F). Stir the mixture

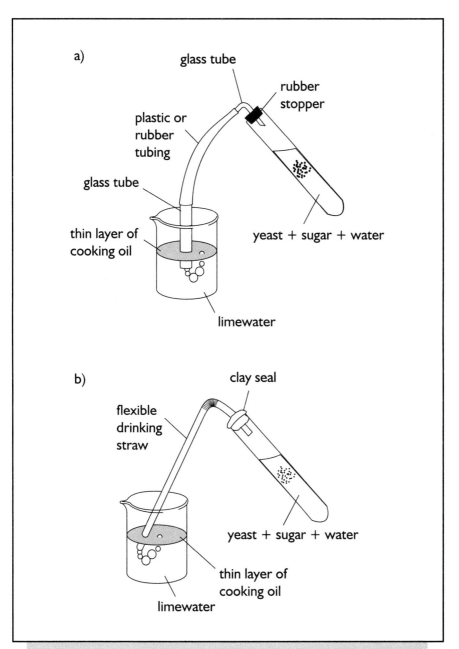

a)

glass tube

rubber stopper

plastic or rubber tubing

glass tube

thin layer of cooking oil

yeast + sugar + water

limewater

b)

clay seal

flexible drinking straw

yeast + sugar + water

thin layer of cooking oil

limewater

Figure 17. Limewater can be used to test for carbon dioxide. Either setup will work for this experiment.

until it is uniform. Add a small quantity of the mixture to a test tube. Place a one-hole rubber stopper with a short length of glass tubing into the tube's mouth. **Ask an adult to help you** insert the glass tubing into the rubber stopper. A drop of cooking oil will serve to lubricate the glass and make insertion easier. Attach a length of plastic or rubber tubing to the end of the glass tubing. It can carry any gas released by the yeast and sugar-water mixture to another piece of glass tubing immersed in a vial containing limewater covered with a thin layer of cooking oil (see Figure 17a). The oil will seal off the limewater from the air, which has a small concentration (0.04 percent) of CO_2.

If you do not have a rubber stopper and glass tubing, you can use a flexible straw in place of the glass tube and clay in place of the stopper, as shown in Figure 17b.

4-2*
Yeast and Different Sugars

For a closer look at how yeast reacts with different sugars, thoroughly mix a package of dry yeast with about 125 mL (1/2 cup) of warm (35°C, or 95°F) water. Pour about 1/3 of the mixture into each of 3 small juice glasses. Tape labels with the words *glucose*, *sucrose*, and *starch* to the glasses, as shown in Figure 18. Place the labeled glasses in a pot that is partially filled with warm (35°C, or 95°F) water. Add a tablespoon of corn syrup to the glass labeled *Glucose*. (Corn syrup contains glucose sugar.) Add a tablespoon of ordinary granulated sugar to the cup labeled *Sucrose*. Add a tablespoon of cornstarch to the remaining glass. Stir each mixture with separate spoons.

Things you will need:

- dry yeast
- water
- measuring cup
- 3 juice glasses
- masking tape
- marking pen
- pot
- tablespoon
- corn syrup
- granulated sugar
- cornstarch
- 3 spoons
- clock or watch
- paper and pen or pencil

Watch the mixtures over the next hour. In which glass do bubbles of carbon dioxide gas appear first? Place one ear near the top of each glass. Can you hear the gas bubbles fizzing and popping? In which container is gas produced at the fastest rate? In which glass do you first smell alcohol? In order to observe the bubbles of gas as they emerge from the mixture, you may have to use a spoon to remove the fine foam of bubbles that forms above the liquid. From the size and rate at which bubbles form, in which glass is the reaction proceeding fastest? Record your observations. Can you explain the results you observe?

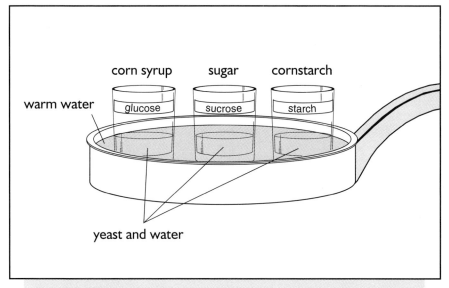

Figure 18. Yeast reacts with carbohydrates to form carbon dioxide and alcohol. Does it react faster with glucose, sucrose, or starch?

Exploring on Your Own

Design an experiment to see what effect salt has on the reaction of yeast with sugar.

Find a recipe for making bread that includes yeast and sugar. Make the bread, then cut it open with a sharp knife. What evidence do you have that a gas was produced during the baking process?

4-3*
Yeast as a Catalyst

Because this experiment involves flames and boiling water, you should work under adult supervision.

Yeast is sometimes used with substances other than foods because it can act as a catalyst. A catalyst is a substance that changes the speed of a chemical reaction without being chemically changed by the reaction. Hydrogen peroxide (H_2O_2) is a chemical that changes slowly into water and oxygen. The reaction can be represented by the following chemical equation:

Things you will need:

- an adult
- 3 percent solution of hydrogen peroxide (from a drugstore)
- small test tube
- rusty nail
- boiling water
- coffee cup
- 12-oz Styrofoam cup
- thermometer
- matches
- candle
- thin piece of wood
- tablespoon
- dry yeast

$$2H_2O_2 \rightarrow 2H_2O + O_2$$

As you probably know, oxygen is a gas that supports combustion. That is, substances such as wood, coal, alcohol, and many other things will burn if oxygen is present. Because air is 21 percent oxygen, these same substances will burn in air. However, they will burn much faster in pure oxygen.

The rate at which hydrogen peroxide breaks down into water and oxygen can be greatly increased by adding a catalyst. To see the effect of a catalyst, pour a few milliliters of a 3-percent solution of hydrogen peroxide into a small test tube. Do you see any evidence, such as the formation of bubbles, of a gas being released?

Place a rusty nail in the liquid and watch it closely for a few minutes. Rust is iron oxide, which can sometimes act as a catalyst. Can you see bubbles of gas collecting on the nail?

97

Pour some boiling water into a coffee cup. Place the test tube in the hot water and observe the peroxide and nail for a few minutes. Does temperature have any effect on the rate at which the liquid decomposes?

To find out if yeast will catalyze the reaction, add about 60 mL (2 oz) of a 3-percent solution of hydrogen peroxide to a 12-oz Styrofoam cup. Place a thermometer in the liquid and measure its temperature. While waiting for the thermometer to reach a steady reading, light a candle and prepare a thin piece of wood about 10 cm (4 in) long that you can use as a glowing splint.

Record the temperature of the hydrogen peroxide solution and remove the thermometer. Then pour a tablespoon of dry yeast into the solution. What happens?

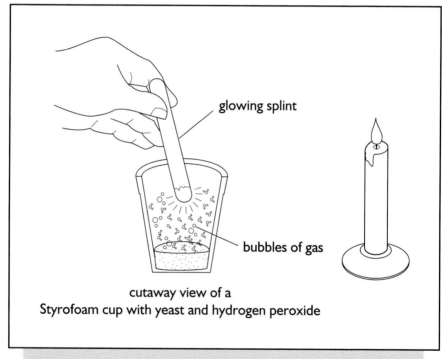

glowing splint

bubbles of gas

cutaway view of a
Styrofoam cup with yeast and hydrogen peroxide

Figure 19. What happens when a glowing splint is placed in the bubbles of gas that form when yeast is added to hydrogen peroxide?

Prepare a glowing splint by placing one end of the thin piece of wood in the candle flame. Let it burn for a few seconds, then blow it out. The splint should be glowing but not burning when you place it in the bubbles of gas forming in the Styrofoam cup, as shown in Figure 19. What happens to the glowing splint? What evidence do you have that oxygen is being produced?

Put the thermometer back in the liquid. What has happened to the temperature of the liquid?

Reactions that produce heat cause an increase in temperature and are called exothermic reactions. Those that absorb heat show a decrease in temperature and are called endothermic reactions. Is the decomposition of hydrogen peroxide an exothermic or an endothermic reaction? What makes you think so?

Exploring on Your Own

Carry out an investigation of catalysts. Where are they used in industry? What catalysts are found in your body and why are they important?

4-4*
Baking Soda

Yeast is not the only ingredient that can be used to produce a gas and make breads and cakes less dense and more appetizing. Baking soda can also be used to produce carbon dioxide. Baking soda, as you can see from the list of ingredients on its box, is 100 percent sodium bicarbonate ($NaHCO_3$).

To see how baking soda can be used to make carbon dioxide, pour about a teaspoon of the powder into a widemouthed glass, jar, or beaker. Then add a few drops of vinegar. What happens?

To see that the gas produced is probably carbon dioxide, which does not burn and will, in fact, smother a fire, repeat the experiment. This time, though, use a small piece of clay to support a birthday candle on the bottom of the vessel, as shown in Figure 20. With **an adult present**, light the candle before you add the vinegar. What happens to the candle flame as the gas produced by the reaction surrounds it?

What evidence do you have to support the idea that carbon dioxide is produced when vinegar is added to baking soda? What could you do to be more certain that the gas is carbon dioxide?

Will any acid react with baking soda to produce the gas? To find out, try adding lemon juice, orange juice, and pickle juice to separate samples of baking soda. Do these acids react with baking soda

Things you will need:

- baking soda
- teaspoon
- widemouthed glass, jar, or beaker
- vinegar
- clay
- birthday candle
- matches
- an adult
- lemon juice
- orange juice
- pickle juice
- Tang crystals
- Kool-Aid crystals
- water
- can of baking powder

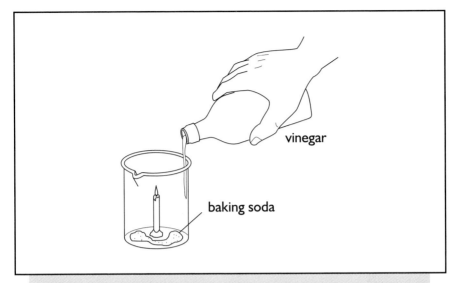

Figure 20. Use a candle flame to find out what gas is produced when baking soda and vinegar are mixed.

to form a gas? Which liquid appears to be the strongest acid? The weakest acid? What makes you think so?

As you found in Chapter 3, some solids such as Tang and Kool-Aid crystals have acidic properties when dissolved in water. To see if these substance will react with baking soda in the same way as vinegar, mix each of these solids with a little baking soda in separate containers. Then add a few drops of water. What do you observe?

As you know, baking soda is sodium bicarbonate. Look at the list of ingredients on a can of baking *powder*. It contains sodium bicarbonate, cornstarch, and a solid acid such as calcium phosphate $[Ca(H_2PO_4)_2]$. Predict what will happen if you add water to a teaspoon of baking powder, then try it. Was your prediction correct? Why do you think many baking recipes call for baking powder?

Exploring on Your Own

Some baking recipes include baking soda rather than baking powder or yeast but no solid acid. In all these recipes, the dough is heated.

101

Could it be that baking soda breaks down and releases carbon dioxide when heated? Design an experiment to find out. Then carry out your experiment **under adult supervision**.

Examine a cookbook. Look for recipes that call for baking soda. Try one of the recipes and see if you can predict what will happen when the ingredients are heated.

Baking soda is sometimes thrown on small fires. Why would anyone add baking soda to a fire?

4-5*
The Many Uses of Baking Soda

In addition to its use in baking, sodium bicarbonate has a variety of purposes. It is used to make other chemicals and is found in many medicines, such as antacids. Because it is a weak base, it can be mixed with water and drunk to relieve acid indigestion. It can be used to soak feet; to clean teeth, shower stalls, tiles, cutting boards, steel knives, combs, and hair brushes; and to absorb odors from refrigerators, clothes hampers, and pet cages. It can soften bathwater, clean silver (see Experiment 3-8), polish chrome, remove corrosion from car batteries, and soften the quills for easier removal from a dog who was too successful in chasing a porcupine. Because it decomposes when heated to form carbon dioxide, it is often spread on oil fires to smother the flames.

Things you will need:

- large plastic jar with a screw-on lid
- small, tall bottle such as an olive jar
- hammer
- nail
- smooth board
- graduated cylinder or measuring cup
- water
- tablespoon
- baking soda
- vinegar
- sink
- soda-acid fire extinguisher
- box of baking soda
- cornstarch
- cooking pan
- cooking oil
- an adult
- stove
- old dinner plate
- cloth
- marking pens or watercolors
- safety goggles

A Baking Soda Fire Extinguisher

Another use of baking soda is in fire extinguishers. As you know from the previous experiment, baking soda, when mixed with an acid, produces carbon dioxide, a gas that can be used to smother

103

fires. To see how such a fire extinguisher works, you can make one from a large plastic jar that has a screw-on lid and a small, tall bottle such as an olive jar.

Remove the lid from the large plastic jar and, **wearing safety goggles**, use a hammer and nail to punch a small hole through it, as shown in Figure 21a. Pour about 500 mL (2 cups) of water into the jar. Add about 2 tablespoons of baking soda and stir the mixture. Be sure the mouth of the smaller empty bottle will be above the level of the solution in the large jar when it is placed in the jar. If such is not the case, pour some of the solution out of the jar.

Nearly fill the smaller bottle with vinegar. Carefully place this bottle on the bottom of the large jar, as shown in Figure 21b. Screw the lid with the hole in it back onto the large jar. Hold the jar next to a sink. Then turn it on its side and point it down into the sink. What happens? Can you explain what you observe?

Read the instructions on a soda-acid fire extinguisher and the ingredients, if listed. After reading, see if you can explain how this kind of fire extinguisher works.

Baking Soda Clay

You can even make your own clay from baking soda. Mix together a 16-oz box of baking soda and a cup of cornstarch in a cooking pan. Then add about 300 mL (1 1/4 cups) of water and a tablespoon of cooking oil. **Under adult supervision**, stir this mixture as you heat it slowly on a stove for about 15 minutes or until it reaches a uniform and moderately thick consistency.

Pour the warm mixture onto an old dinner plate and cover with a damp cloth. After the mixture has cooled, spread cornstarch on a smooth board, place the mixture on the board, and knead it as you would dough until it is smooth. You can use the clay to mold and sculpt a variety of creations. Let the clay dry and then color or paint with marking pens or watercolors.

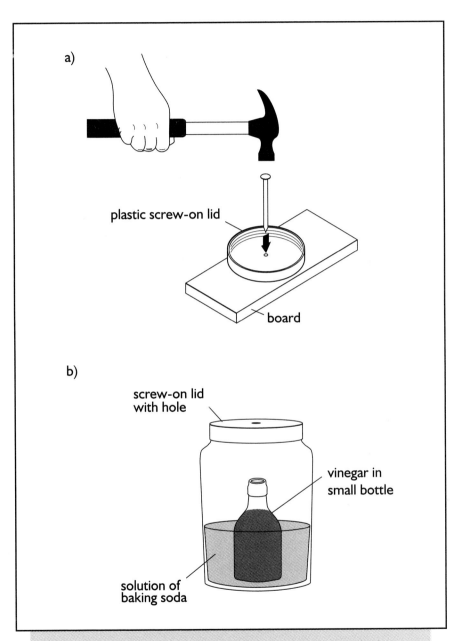

a)

plastic screw-on lid

board

b)

screw-on lid
with hole

vinegar in
small bottle

solution of
baking soda

Figure 21. A simple soda-acid fire extinguisher can be made in your kitchen.

Exploring on Your Own

Look at a variety of containers in your kitchen and bathroom that hold foods and other materials. Check the list of ingredients on these containers. How many contain sodium bicarbonate (baking soda)?

Find out where sodium bicarbonate comes from and what industrial uses it serves.

What is the difference between sodium bicarbonate and sodium carbonate (soda)? Can one be obtained from the other?

5

Experimenting with Solids from the Kitchen

Spaghetti and eggs, when hard-boiled, are two solid foods commonly found in kitchens. In this chapter, they serve as the main ingredients for some unique experiments.

In addition to these solids, you will need some other materials, but they can all be found in your kitchen or in rooms nearby. By the time you complete these experiments, you will realize that spaghetti and eggs are more than just foods. They provide a means of understanding some interesting scientific principles as well.

"Eggsperiments"

Experiments 5-2 through 5-6 involve eggs, a common food found in the kitchen. The outside of an egg is solid, which is why "eggsperiments" are found in this chapter. However, if you have ever dropped a raw egg, you know that an egg is a liquid beneath its shell. On the other hand, a hard-boiled egg is solid throughout.

5-1*
The Tensile Strength of Spaghetti

Normally, we do not think of spaghetti as a strong material. Maybe that is because we usually see it only after it has been softened by cooking. Open a box of spaghetti and you can see that it comes in long, thin, solid strands. On the boxes of some brands, the thickness of the strands is indicated by a number; for example, regular spaghetti is number 8. Buy some spaghetti of different thicknesses. Include some angel hair spaghetti. Determine the tensile strength of each size of spaghetti as described below.

Things you will need:

- spaghetti of different thickness
- 2 tables, chairs, or stacks of books
- heavy books or weights or a partner
- Styrofoam cup
- string
- pennies or identical steel washers
- paper clips
- graph paper
- pencil
- ruler

Tensile strength is measured by stretching an object until it breaks. A rope used in a tug-of-war is under tension. Compression occurs when forces push an object together. For example, a pillar supporting a building is subject to compression. When an object bends, there is both tension and compression, as shown in Figure 22.

To measure the tensile (tension) strength of a length of spaghetti, you can bend it by adding weight to its center until it breaks. Support opposite ends of a single piece of spaghetti with two tables, chairs, or stacks of books. Allow about 2 cm (1 in) at each end to rest on the supports. Place heavy books or other weights on these ends so that the spaghetti cannot move. An even better method would be to have a partner press on the ends of the spaghetti with his or her thumbs.

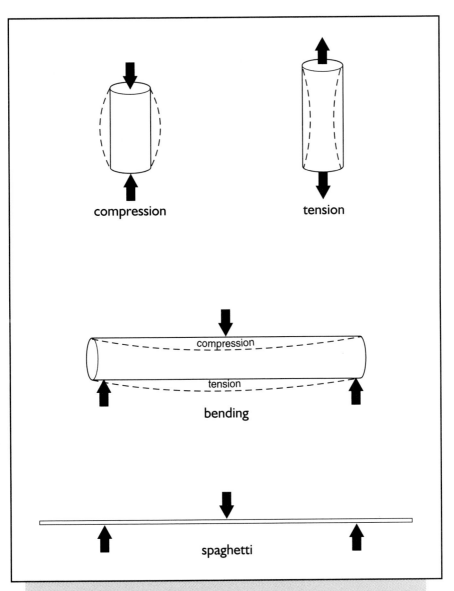

Figure 22. Compression and tension are two types of stress. To measure the tensile strength of spaghetti, you will bend it.

Stress can be applied by hanging a Styrofoam cup from the center of the strand of spaghetti, as shown in Figure 23. Pennies or identical steel washers, used as weights, can be added to the cup. Use one hand to add the weights. Meanwhile, keep your other hand under the cup so that when the spaghetti strand breaks the weights will not be scattered all over the floor.

Begin with a single strand of spaghetti. How many pennies or washers must you add to the cup before the strand breaks?

Repeat the experiment with two strands of spaghetti (Figure 23). Notice that a paper clip is placed at each end to keep the strands together. How many pennies or washers are needed to break two strands? To break three strands? Four strands? Five strands? How is the tensile strength of the spaghetti related to the number of strands you use?

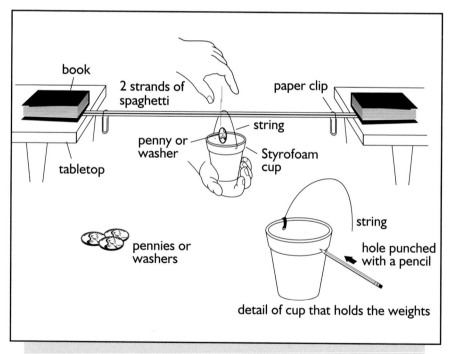

Figure 23. How strong is spaghetti?

Plot a graph of the spaghetti's tensile strength versus the number of strands used. The axes of your graph will resemble those shown in Figure 24. Draw the best line you can through the points you plotted. Does the strength of the spaghetti appear to be proportional to the number of strands used?

Now try a thicker or a thinner type of spaghetti. Again, measure the breaking point of one, two, three, four, and five strands of spaghetti. Does the thickness of the spaghetti affect its tensile strength?

Plot your data for the second experiment on the same graph you used before. How do the graphs compare?

Does the shape of the strands affect the strength? For example, are flat strands stronger than round ones?

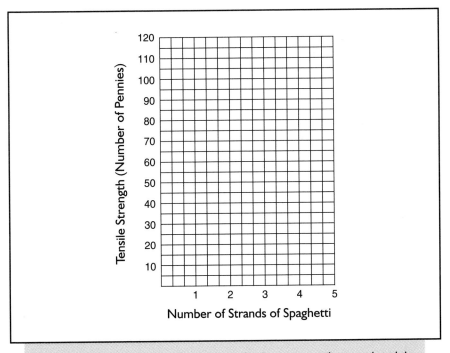

Figure 24. Plot a graph to show the relationship between tensile strength and the number of strands of spaghetti.

Does the length of the unsupported part of the strand or strands affect the tensile strength of the spaghetti? For example, is the force required to break a 10 cm span greater than the force to break a 20 cm span? If it is, is it twice as great?

Exploring on Your Own

Investigate the tensile strength of toothpicks. Investigate the role of tensile strength in architecture.

5-2
Eggs and the Equinoxes

Many people believe that a raw egg can be balanced on end, as shown in Figure 25, only at the time of an equinox—around the 20th of March or September, when the sun is directly above Earth's equator. To test this idea,

Things you will need:

- dish towel
- kitchen counter
- raw egg
- calendar

spread out a dish towel on a kitchen counter. Then try to balance an egg on one end while it rests on the towel. This will require patience, but if you succeed in balancing an egg at some time other than the equinox, you have disproven this widely held belief. If you fail to balance the egg no matter how hard you try, repeat the experiment at the time of an equinox. If you succeed at that time, you have added credence to the belief. What are your results?

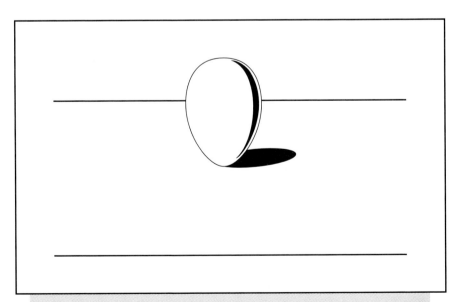

Figure 25. Can an egg be balanced on end only during an equinox?

5-3*
Evidence from a Spinning Egg

If someone hands you an egg, you cannot tell by looking whether it is hard-boiled or uncooked. But there is a way to find out. Put the egg on a kitchen counter and make it spin.

Things you will need:
• kitchen counter
• raw egg
• hard-boiled egg

Place your finger near one end of the egg so that it stops spinning. Then quickly remove your finger. Does the egg continue to move or does it remain at rest?

To find out what the result of this experiment means, try it with a raw egg and then with a hard-boiled egg. Which egg continues to move after being stopped? Why does one egg continue to move after being stopped and the other does not? It might help to think about what happens to you when a car in which you are riding stops suddenly. What would happen if you were not wearing a seat belt?

Did you have trouble understanding why one egg remains at rest while the other continues to move? If you did, go to the library or a physical science textbook and read about Newton's laws of motion, especially his first law of motion.

Can you think of at least one practical way that you could use what you have learned in this experiment?

Exploring on Your Own

Investigate how Newton's first law of motion applies to motion on Earth and in space.

5-4*
Eggs in Water and Salt Water

Put an uncooked egg in half a glass of water. Does the egg float or sink? What does this tell you about the density of an egg as compared with the density of water?

Next, in another glass prepare a saturated solution of ordinary table salt. You can do this by adding salt to half a glass of water and stirring until no

Things you will need:
- uncooked egg
- several drinking glasses
- water
- table salt
- spoon or other stirring device
- food coloring
- graduated cylinder or measuring cup
- seawater (optional)

more salt will dissolve. Carefully pour most of the salt solution into another glass, leaving the undissolved salt behind.

Add a drop or two of food coloring to the salt solution so that it can be distinguished from the water in the first glass with the egg.

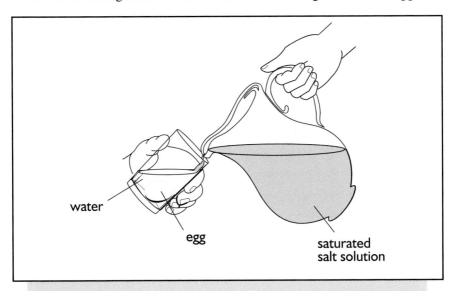

water

egg

saturated
salt solution

Figure 26. Where will the egg be after the salt solution is poured into the glass with water?

Pour the colored solution into a measuring cup. Then tip the glass of water that holds the egg at an angle and slowly pour the colored salt solution down the side of the glass, as shown in Figure 26. In view of the relative densities of water and the salt solution (see Experiment 1-4), where do you expect the salt solution to go?

After you have poured some of the salt solution into the water, where is the egg? What can you say now about the density of an egg? If you had to estimate the density of an egg, what range of values would you give, based on the data you have collected here and in Experiment 1-4?

If you live near the ocean, find the density of seawater. Then place an egg in the seawater. Does it sink or float? What additional information does this provide about the density of an egg?

Exploring on Your Own

How would you go about finding the actual density of an egg? Do brown eggs and white eggs have different densities?

5-5
An Egg, a Bottle, and Air Pressure

Things you will need:

- medium or large eggs
- one-liter or one-quart glass bottle with narrow neck
- an adult
- cooking pan
- balloon
- hot tap water
- cold water
- cooking oil
- sheet of paper
- matches
- sink

For this experiment, you will need some hard-boiled eggs and a large glass bottle with a mouth slightly smaller than the diameter of a hard-boiled egg. **Ask an adult** to help you boil several eggs in a pan. The eggs should cook in the boiling water for at least 10 minutes.

While the eggs are cooking, pull the mouth of an empty balloon over the mouth of a one-liter or one-quart glass bottle. Place the bottle in a pan of hot tap water. What happens to the air in the bottle? How can you tell?

Remove the balloon and let some hot tap water flow into the bottle. Swish the water around inside the bottle so as to warm the air inside. Do this several times. Then put the empty balloon back on the bottle and place the bottle in a pan of cold water. What happens to the balloon as the air inside the bottle cools? What does the balloon's behavior tell you about what happens to air when it cools?

After the eggs have cooked, **ask an adult** to remove the pan from the stove, pour off the hot water, and add cold water. Let the eggs cool in the cold water. When they are cool, remove their shells.

Find an egg that is just slightly larger than the mouth of the bottle. Put a little cooking oil on your finger and rub it around the inside rim of the bottle's mouth. This will reduce the friction between the egg and the glass. Next, fold a quarter of a sheet of paper accordion-like, as shown in Figure 27a. **Ask an adult** to light the paper and drop it into the bottle. As soon as the paper enters the bottle, place the hard-boiled egg on the mouth of the bottle

117

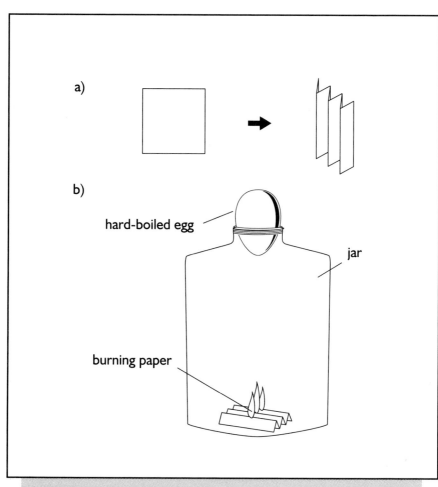

a)

b)

hard-boiled egg

jar

burning paper

Figure 27. a) Fold a quarter sheet of paper in accordion fashion. b) **Have an adult light the paper and drop it into a large bottle.** Place the hard-boiled, peeled egg on the bottle's mouth and watch.

(Figure 27b). Why does the egg bob up and down as it rests on the bottle above the burning paper? What happens to the egg when the flame goes out?

What did the burning paper do to the air in the bottle? What happened to the air in the bottle after the flame went out? Why do you think the egg did what it did?

Can you think of a way to get the egg out of the bottle? If not, try this: Fill the bottle with water and turn it upside down over the sink. Put your finger into the neck of the bottle to hold up the egg so that the water and remains of the burned paper can fall into the sink. Next, with the bottle upside down and the egg in its neck, place your mouth next to the mouth of the bottle and blow as hard as you can. When you stop blowing, the egg will fall out of the bottle. Can you explain why?

5-6
An Egg in an Acid

Put an uncooked egg in a glass and cover it with water. Put a second uncooked egg in a glass and cover it with vinegar, which, as you know, is an acid. Notice that both eggs sink to the bottom of the liquids. In which liquid do you see bubbles of gas forming on the egg's shell? In which liquid do you soon find that the egg is floating? What do you think has made the egg float?

To see a somewhat similar effect, drop some raisins into a

Things you will need:

- uncooked eggs
- drinking glasses
- water
- vinegar
- raisins
- ginger ale or seltzer
- sink
- bowl
- 2 small glasses, vials, or test tubes
- calcium carbonate (limestone) chips

glass of ginger ale or seltzer. Why do the raisins rise to the surface? Unlike the egg in vinegar, the raisins, after rising to the surface, fall back into the liquid. How can you explain the difference in behavior between the raisins and the egg?

Leave the eggs in the liquids overnight. Then pour off the liquids. Feel the surface of the two eggs. Which egg has lost its shell? What do you think happened to the shell?

The shell-less egg has a rubbery feel. Do you think it will bounce like a rubber ball? To find out, hold the egg about 5 cm (2 in) above the bottom of a sink and drop it. Does it bounce? What happens as you gradually increase the height from which you drop it?

Break an egg into a bowl and collect the pieces of its shell, rinse them off with water, and drop half of them into each of two small glasses, vials, or test tubes. Put the bowl with the raw egg into the refrigerator so that it can be used later. Add enough vinegar to cover the pieces of shell in one glass or test tube. Add water to the second sample of eggshells. In which glass or tube is there evidence of a chemical reaction? What is the evidence? **After working with raw eggs, wash your hands thoroughly with soap and warm water**.

You may have heard that eggshells are made of calcium carbonate ($CaCO_3$), which is also a major component of your bones and of limestone. If possible, add a few calcium carbonate (limestone) chips to a small glass, vial, or test tube. Then add a few milliliters of vinegar. Does vinegar react with the calcium carbonate as it did with the eggshells? Does the addition of vinegar to calcium carbonate support the idea that eggshells are made of calcium carbonate? Does it prove it?

Further Reading

Adams, Richard, and Robert Gardner. *Ideas for Science Projects.* Revised Edition. Danbury, Conn.: Franklin Watts, 1997.

Bochinski, Julianne Blair. *The Complete Handbook of Science Fair Projects.* New York: John Wiley & Sons, 1996.

Bombaugh, Ruth. *Science Fair Success, Revised and Expanded.* Springfield, N.J.: Enslow Publishers, Inc., 1999.

Cobb, Vicki. *More Science Experiments You Can Eat.* New York: HarperCollins Children's Books, 1984.

Gardner, Robert. *Science Fair Projects—Planning, Preparing, Succeeding.* Springfield, N.J.: Enslow Publishers, Inc., 1999.

———. *More Ideas for Science Projects.* New York: Franklin Watts, Inc., 1989.

———. *Science Projects About Chemistry.* Hillside, N.J.: Enslow Publishers, Inc., 1994.

Herbert, Don. *Mr. Wizard's Supermarket Science.* New York: Random House, 1980.

Krieger, Melanie Jacobs. *How to Excel in Science Competitions, Revised and Updated.* Springfield, N.J.: Enslow Publishers, Inc., 1999.

Loeschnig, Louis V. *Simple Chemistry Experiments with Everyday Materials.* New York: Sterling Publishing Company, 1995.

Markle, Sandra. *The Young Scientist's Guide to Successful Science Projects.* New York: Lothrop, Lee, & Shepard, 1990.

Mebane, R., and T. R. Rybolt. *Adventures with Atoms and Molecules, Book I: Chemistry Experiments for Young People.* Springfield, N.J.: Enslow Publishers, Inc., 1985.

————. *Adventures with Atoms and Molecules, Book II: Chemistry Experiments for Young People*. Springfield, N.J.: Enslow Publishers, Inc., 1987.

————. *Adventures with Atoms and Molecules, Book III: Chemistry Experiments for Young People*. Springfield, N.J.: Enslow Publishers, Inc., 1991.

————. *Adventures with Atoms and Molecules, Book IV: Chemistry Experiments for Young People*. Springfield, N.J.: Enslow Publishers, Inc., 1992.

————. *Adventures with Atoms and Molecules, Book V: Chemistry Experiments for Young People*. Springfield, N.J.: Enslow Publishers, Inc., 1995.

Newton, David E. *Making and Using Scientific Equipment*. New York: Franklin Watts, 1993.

Rosner, Marc Alan. *Science Fair Success Using the Internet*. Springfield, N.J.: Enslow Publishers, Inc., 1999.

Tocci, Salvatore. *How to Do a Science Fair Project*. Revised Edition. Danbury, Conn.: Franklin Watts, 1997.

VanCleave, Janice P. *Chemistry for Every Kid: One Hundred and One Easy Experiments that Really Work*. New York: John Wiley & Sons, Inc., 1989.

Internet Addresses

Miami Museum of Science. "The pH Factor." n.d. <http://www.miamisci.org/ph/default.html> (November 17, 1998).

Rader New Media. *Chem4Kids.com*. "Acids and Bases Are Everywhere." 1998. <http://chem4kids.com/chem4kids/reactions/acidbase.html> (November 17, 1998).

List of Suppliers

Carolina Biological Supply Co.
2700 York Road
Burlington, NC 27215
(800) 334-5551
http://www.carolina.com

Central Scientific Co. (CENCO)
3300 CENCO Parkway
Franklin Park, IL 60131
(800) 262-3626
http://www.cenconet.com

Connecticut Valley Biological Supply Co., Inc.
82 Valley Road
P.O. Box 326
Southampton, MA 01073
(800) 628-7748

Delta Education
P.O. Box 915
Hudson, NH 03051-0915
(800) 258-1302

Edmund Scientific Co.
101 East Gloucester Pike
Barrington, NJ 08007
(609) 547-3488

Fisher Science Education
485 S. Frontage Road
Burr Ridge, IL 60521
(800) 955-4663
http://www.fisheredu.com

Frey Scientific
100 Paragon Parkway
Mansfield, OH 44905
(800) 225-3739

Nasco-Modesto
P.O. Box 3837
Modesto, CA 95352-3837
(800) 558-9595
http://www.nasco.com

Nasco Science
P.O. Box 901
Fort Atkinson, WI 53538-0901
(800) 558-9595

Sargent-Welch/VWR Scientific
911 Commerce Court
Buffalo Grove, IL 60089-2375
(800) 727-4368
http://www.SargentWelch.com

Science Kit & Boreal Laboratories
777 East Park Drive
Tonawanda, NY 14150-6782
(800) 828-7777
http://sciencekit.com

Wards Natural Science Establishment, Inc.
5100 West Henrietta Road
P.O. Box 92912
Rochester, NY 14692-9012
(800) 962-2660
http://www.wardsci.com

Index